LAWRENCE OF ARABIA

LEADERSHIP ▪ STRATEGY ▪ CONFLICT

DAVID MURPHY ▪ ILLUSTRATED BY GIUSEPPE RAVA

First published in 2011 by Osprey Publishing
Midland House, West Way, Botley, Oxford OX2 0PH, UK
44-02 23rd St, Suite 219, Long Island City, NY 11101, USA

E-mail: info@ospreypublishing.com

OSPREY PUBLISHING IS PART OF THE OSPREY GROUP

ISBN: 978 1 84908 368 3
E-book ISBN: 978 1 84908 369 0

Editorial by Ilios Publishing Ltd, Oxford, UK
Cartography: Mapping Specialists Ltd
Design: Myriam Bell Design, France
Index by David Worthington
Originated by PDQ Digital Media Solutions, Suffolk, UK
Printed in China through Worldprint Ltd

11 12 13 14 15   10 9 8 7 6 5 4 3 2 1

www.ospreypublishing.com

Acknowledgements

Many people have offered help and advice during my research for this book. Once again, I am indebted to Lieutenant-Colonel Mesut Uyar of the Turkish Military Academy for expert information on the Ottoman Army. My thanks also go to Lieutenant Alan Kearney of the Irish Defence Forces and Dr Nathalie Genet-Rouffiac of the Service Historique de la Défense. I would like to acknowledge the help of Professor Norman Stone and the assistance of the staff at the Imperial War Museum, the Tate Gallery, the Bodleian Library and the Library of Congress.

I am particularly indebted to several members of the T. E. Lawrence Society, including Peter Leney, Ian Heritage, Philip Neale and Brian Duggan. I owe a huge debt of gratitude to Aisling Dunne of the Irish Architectural Archive. My thanks also go to Marcus Cowper and Christopher Pannell at Ilios Publishing – their patience was much appreciated. I'd also like to thank Giuseppe Rava for the wonderful artwork he has produced for this book. Finally, thanks and appreciation go to Rachel McDonald and to my sister, Sharon.

Artist's note

Readers may care to note that the original paintings from which the colour plates in this book were prepared are available for private sale. All reproduction copyright whatsoever is retained by the Publishers. All enquiries should be addressed to:

Giuseppe Rava,
via Borgotto 17,
48018 FAENZA (RA),
ITALY

Email: info@g-rava.it
Website: www.g-rava.it

The Publishers regret that they can enter into no correspondence upon this matter.

Cover image

Imperial War Museum, Q73534.

The Imperial War Museum Collections

Some of the photos in this book come from the Imperial War Museum's huge collections, which cover all aspects of conflict involving Britain and the Commonwealth since the start of the 20th century. These rich resources are available online to search, browse and buy at www.iwmcollections.org.uk. In addition to collections online, you can visit the visitor rooms where you can explore over 8 million photographs, thousands of hours of moving images, the largest sound archive of its kind in the world, thousands of diaries and letters written by people in wartime, and a huge reference library. To make an appointment, call (020) 7416 5320, or e-mail mail@iwm.org.uk.

Imperial War Museum www.iwm.org.uk

The Woodland Trust

Osprey Publishing are supporting the Woodland Trust, the UK's leading woodland conservation charity, by funding the dedication of trees.

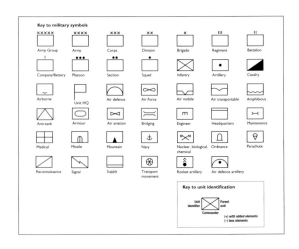

CONTENTS

INTRODUCTION

Thomas Edward Lawrence (1888–1935), later known as 'Lawrence of Arabia'. He is photographed here in Aqaba in 1917, wearing Arab robes. This is how most modern enthusiasts of the Arab Revolt imagine him. (IWM Q59314)

Thomas Edward Lawrence (1888–1935), or 'Lawrence of Arabia' as he is more commonly known, remains one of the most iconic figures of the 20th century. Despite not being a career soldier, his World War I exploits had a major impact on the outcome of the war. Indeed, this amateur soldier was to play a crucial role in the creation of the modern Middle East. Nothing in his early life suggested that he would excel in a military career. At the outbreak of the war, Lawrence (usually known as 'Ned' to his family and friends) seemed destined for a career as an archaeologist. To those close to him, he also confessed a desire to embark on a career in writing or publishing. Having volunteered for service in 1914, Lawrence served in relative obscurity until 1916. The Arab Revolt that broke out that year served to catapult Lawrence into a more dramatic phase of military activity. Eventually he would find himself in the full glare of the public spotlight because of his wartime exploits. By the end of the war he had been promoted to full colonel and had been highly decorated. Most of his contemporaries were certain that an influential military or political career lay ahead. Instead, Lawrence chose obscurity, adding fuel to the growing public fascination with him and ensuring his status as one of the most enigmatic figures of his time.

Lawrence was an extraordinary man by any analysis, and he found himself in the midst of extraordinary events. Once posted to Arabia in 1916, he displayed an uncanny ability to assess the various Arab leaders and later to

Opposite: At the outbreak of World War I the Ottoman Empire retained considerable possessions in Europe, Asia and Arabia. These bordered Russia, Persia and British Protectorates in Aden, Kuwait and Bahrain. While Allied forces advanced into Ottoman territory from 1914, the campaigns in locations such as the Sinai, Gallipoli and Mesopotamia did not fare well, while Ottoman control of its possessions in Arabia remained intact. In the months before the outbreak of the Arab Revolt in 1916, Ottoman commanders reinforced their garrisons in Arabia while the main Arab forces gathered near Mecca and Medina.

The Ottoman Empire, 1914

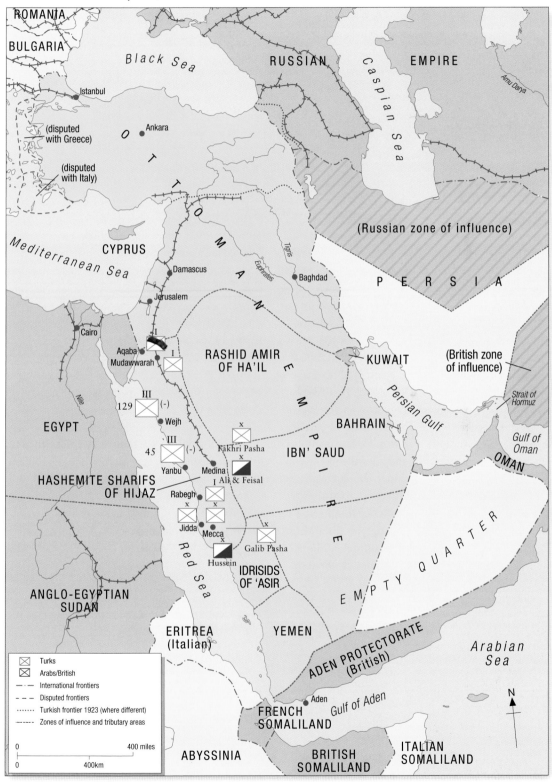

ROMANIA

BULGARIA

Black Sea

RUSSIAN

Caspian Sea

EMPIRE

Amu Darya

Istanbul

(disputed
with Greece)

Ankara

O T T O M A N

(disputed
with Italy)

Mediterranean Sea

CYPRUS

Tigris

(Russian zone of influence)

Euphrates

Damascus

Baghdad

P E R S I A

Jerusalem

Cairo

Aqaba

I

Mudawwarah

I

RASHID AMIR
OF HA'IL

E M P I R E

KUWAIT

(British zone
of influence)

129

III

(-)

BAHRAIN

Persian Gulf

Strait of
Hormuz

EGYPT

Wejh

x

Gulf of
Oman

45

III

(-)

Fakhri Pasha

IBN' SAUD

OMAN

Yanbu

Medina

x

HASHEMITE SHARIFS
OF HIJAZ

Rabegh

I

Ali & Feisal

x

x

Jidda

Mecca

x

Galib Pasha

Red Sea

Hussein

IDRISIDS
OF 'ASIR

E M P T Y   Q U A R T E R

ANGLO-EGYPTIAN
SUDAN

ERITREA
(Italian)

YEMEN

ADEN PROTECTORATE
(British)

*Arabian
Sea*

N

FRENCH
SOMALILAND

Aden

Gulf of Aden

ABYSSINIA

BRITISH
SOMALILAND

ITALIAN
SOMALILAND

Turks

Arabs/British

International frontiers

Disputed frontiers

Turkish frontier 1923 (where different)

Zones of influence and tributary areas

0 — 400 miles

0 — 400km

Lawrence on one of his Brough motorcycles, taken at RAF Cranwell. During World War I he emerged from relative obscurity and became one of the iconic figures of the 20th century. He would seek obscurity once again in his later life. (Bodleian Library, Oxford).

encourage them to support the Allied vision for the direction of the revolt. Above all, Lawrence showed himself to have an almost instinctive grasp of guerrilla warfare. While he had little formal military training, he identified correctly his enemy's weaknesses and devised the best tactics to adopt in attack.

Two of Lawrence's brothers were to die on the Western Front and, although spared the horror of the attritional warfare in that theatre of operations, he emerged from the war profoundly damaged. He retained hopes for greater Arab independence, and the disappointments of the post-war peace conferences exacerbated his personal problems. He had effectively withdrawn from active public life by 1922. Seeking obscurity in the RAF, he later devoted himself to other projects such as the development of high-speed rescue craft for the RAF. Lawrence was also obsessed with speed, and he owned a series of supercharged Brough motorcycles during the 1920s and 1930s. He had been retired from the RAF for just a few months at the time of his death in 1935.

Few, if any, of the commanders of World War I have enjoyed such continued interest after their deaths. This unlikely scholar-soldier has continued to fascinate with hardly a year passing without a new study of his life being published. Indeed, so much has now been written that it is becoming increasingly difficult to get a true sense of Lawrence the man, made doubly difficult by Lawrence's own complex personality. In purely military terms, he has been recognized as an expert commander of unconventional and guerrilla operations. Perhaps unsurprisingly, Lawrence's career has come under the spotlight again in more recent times as coalition forces have struggled to deal with insurgencies in Iraq and Afghanistan. Although Lawrence fought in a totally different world context, he still has something to offer in his military and political assessments. A new generation of professional soldiers have begun to study the career and writings of this unashamedly amateur soldier.

THE EARLY YEARS

Thomas Edward Lawrence was born in Tramadoc in North Wales on 16 August 1888. He was born in the final decades of the Victorian era in family circumstances that were far from orthodox. His father was Sir Thomas Robert Tighe Chapman of South Hill, Delvin, Co. Westmeath in Ireland. This Anglo-Irish gentleman was the product of a distinguished family that had lived in Ireland since the Elizabethan plantations. Lawrence's mother was Sarah Lawrence, a Scottish-born governess who had entered Sir Thomas

Chapman's household in 1879 to serve as nanny and governess to his four daughters. It is not known when the couple began their affair, but Chapman would eventually leave his wife, his children and his ancestral home to run away with Sarah Lawrence. Together they would have five sons: Montagu Robert (1885), Thomas Edward (1888), William George (1889), Frank (1893) and Arnold Walter (1900).

Chapman was never divorced from his wife, so he and Sarah were never married. The couple assumed Sarah's surname and lived as 'Mr and Mrs Lawrence' at various locations before settling in Oxford in 1896, where they bought a house on Polstead Road. Lawrence would later light-heartedly claim to have known of his parents' circumstances, and therefore his own illegitimacy, from boyhood. It is unclear at what date he truly did find this out and it would appear that this facet of his life troubled him deeply.

Lawrence's early years in Oxford do not seem to have been totally unhappy, however. In 1896 he entered the City of Oxford High School, where he continued his education until 1907. He proved himself to be an intelligent, although not brilliant, student. Unlike many of his peers, he abhorred team sports, preferring to engage in more solitary pursuits such as canoeing and cycling. In stature, he would never be impressive, measuring just less than 5ft 6in. (168cm) in height. He did however possess considerable strength and powers of endurance, and these qualities would stand to him during his wartime career.

Above: A previously unpublished photograph of the Chapman family residence: South Hill, Delvin, Co. Westmeath. Lawrence's father, Sir Thomas Chapman, left this estate in order to be with Sarah Lawrence, the governess to his children. The woman in this photograph remains unidentified at this time but may have been Elizabeth Chapman, the deserted wife of Sir Thomas Chapman, or one of his four daughters. (Irish Architectural Archive)

Left: Sarah Lawrence photographed c.1895 with her first four sons. The 'Lawrences' were then living at Langley Lodge in Fawley, on the edge of the New Forest. From left to right, Thomas Edward, Will, Sarah with Frank in her arms and Bob. A fifth son, Arnold ('Arnie'), was born in 1900. (Bodleian Library, Oxford)

As a youth, he never considered a career in the military. Fascinated with archaeology and history, he seemed destined to follow an academic career. He travelled to local sites of historical interest and, during a programme of rebuilding in Oxford, collected pieces of interest from workmen that he later presented to the Ashmolean Museum, beginning a long association with that institution. To family and friends he also confessed to an ambition to start a career in fine printing. He was an adventurous traveller, spending the summers of 1906 and 1907 in France studying castles. The initial expeditions he undertook were with his father, but he would later travel alone. Also, around 1905–06, it is believed that he may have run away from home following an argument and joined the Royal Garrison Artillery in Cornwall. His father seems to have bought him out of this enlistment.

In 1907 he entered Jesus College, University of Oxford, where he continued his studies in medieval castles. He returned to France in the summer of 1908 and, in the summer of 1909, travelled to Syria to examine some of the surviving crusader castles there. Equipped with just a basic rucksack and a camera, he carried out a walking tour through Syria and Palestine and covered over 1,770km (1,100 miles), an enterprise of considerable risk at that time. He was shot at on at least one occasion and on another his death was reported in the Aleppo newspapers. These research trips fuelled his BA thesis, entitled *The Influence of the Crusades on European Military Architecture – to the end of the XIIth century*. In his thesis he convincingly argued that developments in the east had influenced European castle building rather than vice versa, which had previously been argued as being the case. For this research he was awarded a first-class honours degree in 1910. He then returned to the Middle East, spending a period at Jebail in modern-day Lebanon, where he took classes in Arabic. His time at university was also marked by eccentric behaviour of various kinds and he amazed fellow students when he joined the university's Officer Training Corps, where he proved himself to be both a crack shot and an effective scout.

Lawrence photographed with Leonard Woolley at the archaeological dig at Carchemish in modern-day Syria, then Ottoman territory. Lawrence worked on this British Museum excavation between 1911 and 1914 and also spent a period on a dig in Egypt. During this time he gained knowledge of this area and also of Arab languages and tribal customs. This experience would be of use to him during the Arab Revolt. (IWM Q73536)

Increasingly, the focus of his gaze was turning to the Middle East, and in November 1910 he was fortunate enough to be given a job on the British Museum's archaeological dig at Carchemish in Syria, where he worked under D. G. Hogarth of the Ashmolean Museum. He travelled to Syria in early 1911 and, apart from a brief period in England in 1913, he would spend most of the next four years in the Middle East, engaged in archaeological work. Throughout this time he worked in the territory of the Ottoman Empire, a power that by the end

of 1914 would be at war with Britain. As a result he gained much practical knowledge that would later be of use during his wartime career.

During his initial period at Carchemish he not only furthered his archaeological career but also improved his knowledge of Arabic. His work as an overseer of the excavations at Carchemish gave him an invaluable insight into the sensibilities and customs of the Arab workmen. All of this would later stand him in good stead. Lawrence also used Carchemish as a base for further exploration, travelling to northern Mesopotamia (modern-day Iraq) in 1911. It has often been suggested that he was already working as a spy at this time and it is reasonably certain that he carried out a reconnaissance of the section of the Berlin–Baghdad Railway near Carchemish that was being built by German engineers. While difficult to prove, it is certain that Lawrence gained much experience of a region that he would later revisit in wartime.

After a short period working with the distinguished archaeologist Flinders Petrie, Lawrence returned to Carchemish in March 1912. In 1913 he returned to England for a short stay in Oxford, taking two of his Arab friends, Dahoum and Hamoudi, for a visit.

Lawrence's real introduction to the world of military intelligence came in January 1914 when he and his colleague, Leonard Woolley, were invited to join a survey of the Sinai Peninsula. In appearance, this survey was an entirely non-military in nature and had been organized by the Palestine Exploration Fund. In reality it had been ordered by the director of military operations in London; it was to assess the possibilities of the Ottoman Army attacking through the Sinai towards Suez, and also the difficulties that would be faced by a British force operating in that area. Lawrence and Woolley acted as the civilian 'cover', while the expedition was actually led by Captain Stewart Newcombe, who would later serve with Lawrence in Arabia. While Lawrence enjoyed this period of amateur cloak-and-dagger, as it offered an opportunity to visit Petra, he also gained real experience in military planning and surveying. He was also now known to intelligence officers in Cairo and, on Lawrence volunteering for service in 1914, they would make use of his skills and experience.

As the clouds of war gathered, the dig at Carchemish was wound down and Lawrence returned to England. He spent some time working up the archaeological findings of the Sinai expedition with Woolley, and these were published as *The Wilderness of Zin* (1914). On the outbreak of war he joined the Geographical Section of the General Staff (Intelligence) based in the War Office in London. This was initially in a civilian capacity, but on 26 October he was gazetted into the army as a second lieutenant on the 'Special List' – a category reserved for officers with no regimental attachment and hence bound for special duties. Just a few days later, the Ottoman Empire entered

Captain (later Lieutenant-Colonel) Stewart Newcombe, Royal Engineers. In January and February 1914, Lawrence accompanied Newcombe to carry out a survey of Sinai. While this expedition was technically for the Palestine Exploration Fund, in reality it was for intelligence purposes. Lawrence would later serve again with Newcombe on the intelligence staff in Cairo. (IWM Q58908)

the war on the side of Germany and Austro-Hungary. By December 1914 Lawrence was in Cairo, where he joined the Intelligence Department. The territory where he had travelled and worked as an archaeologist belonged to a power that was now at war with England. It was hoped that Lawrence could play his part in the campaign against the Ottoman Empire by employing his knowledge of the languages, tribes and terrain of these areas. No one, not even Lawrence himself, could have suspected that he would play so great a role in the campaigns that were to follow.

THE MILITARY LIFE

Lawrence would have been the first to admit that he was a rank amateur in all things military. Although he had served with the Officer Training Corps when studying as an undergraduate, he never planned on a military career. As a young man with a temporary commission he travelled to Cairo in December 1914, where he joined the intelligence staff at GHQ (general headquarters). The next two years were mixed with periods of excitement and humdrum routine, but during this time he obtained a firm grounding in intelligence work and also proved himself to be a natural practitioner in this field.

When Lawrence arrived in Cairo, the intelligence section at GHQ was being expanded. Rooms were taken at the Savoy Hotel to accommodate the growing number of staff. GHQ had maintained a small intelligence staff before the war but by 1918 this had been expanded to over 700 people. Lawrence served under Colonel Gilbert 'Bertie' Clayton, whose second in command was Major (later Colonel) Stewart Newcombe, with whom Lawrence had explored the Sinai earlier in 1914. During the course of the war, the section was responsible for intelligence reporting to a succession of commanders. These included General Sir John Maxwell (1914–15), General Sir Archibald Murray (1915–17) and finally General Sir Edmund Allenby (1917–18), with whom Lawrence would work closely. The intelligence staff also reported to Sir Reginald Wingate, governor-general of the Sudan. Reports from Cairo's intelligence team were also processed back to London to Lieutenant-General Sir George Macdonagh, director of military intelligence at the War Office. There were also other intelligence agencies at work. The Royal Navy operated its own intelligence section, as did the British High Commission. Additionally, in 1915 the French established an intelligence headquarters, based on Arwad Island off the Libyan coast.

Lawrence began the war attached to the intelligence staff in Cairo, serving as a temporary second lieutenant. He found his early duties quite routine but felt he was performing a more crucial role after his assignment as a liaison officer to the Arab Army in October 1916. He is photographed here after his promotion to captain. (IWM Q59314A)

The intelligence department in Cairo was full of unusual personalities, many of them only recently commissioned, as Lawrence had been. In this new military world Lawrence's appearance was often sloppy. He did not go in for military presentation and regular officers often remarked on the state of his uniform and his general air of untidiness. In this over-populated and hectic intelligence environment, Lawrence established himself as an eccentric but also useful officer. The intelligence section was split into two subsections. Section 1a, commanded by Newcombe, concerned itself with gathering material on the enemy – formations, plans, intentions and the condition of the Ottoman Army. Section 1b was GHQ's counter-intelligence branch. During the course of the next two years, Lawrence would have a number of responsibilities. In June 1915 he described his average day: 'Well, drawing, and overseeing the drawing of maps: overseeing the printing and packing of same; sitting in an office coding and decoding telegrams, interviewing prisoners, writing reports, and giving information from 9am till 7pm.'

This description is consistent with his later comments on life in Section 1a and, although it sounds like a life of boring routine, he seems to be underplaying the important work that he did. One of his primary tasks was compiling profiles of Ottoman military and political leaders and writing reports on the Ottoman territories. These were written in a typical Lawrentian style – a style that some found profoundly irritating. Indeed, his profiles often have a tone similar to that found in John Aubrey's *Brief Lives*, a work he would have been familiar with since his college days. Yet his profiles of senior Ottoman figures contained much information and showed a keen insight into human nature. They were circulated widely in Cairo and also as far as London.

His language skills and knowledge of tribal issues made him an ideal officer for interviewing prisoners. A steady trickle of these came to Cairo: soldiers who had deserted or had been picked up in desert skirmishes. Following the failed Ottoman offensive against the Suez Canal, the number of Turkish POWs increased in number and Lawrence was kept busy. He preferred a friendly, ingratiating style and found that, on showing that he had knowledge of Ottoman territories in Palestine and Syria, these prisoners often talked quite freely, especially Arab tribesmen who had been conscripted. These interrogations allowed him to build up a picture of conditions and morale in the Ottoman Army. Prisoners spoke of poor pay, food and medical facilities, and they also complained of poor leadership and the growing influence of Germany. While much of this was accurate, it must also be said that Lawrence formed an over-optimistic impression of the possibilities of a widespread mutiny of Arab troops in the Ottoman Army.

At the same time, while Lawrence and his brother officers were not directly engaged in counter-intelligence, they became increasingly aware of Turko-German efforts to foment rebellion in Egypt, which was, after all, a somewhat unwilling 'protectorate' of Britain. Throughout 1915 and 1916

Sharif Hussein ibn Ali, the Sharif of Mecca. Sharif Hussein had been in contact with GHQ in Cairo since 1914 and he instigated the revolt in June 1916. One of Lawrence's chief duties was to identify which of the sharif's sons would be most suited to enlarge the scope of the revolt. (IWM Q59888)

Lawrence monitored the general feeling in Cairo and the Egyptian Army as the enemy mounted a campaign designed at promoting rebellion.

Early in 1915, Lawrence had also witnessed the preparations (such as they were) for the planned expedition to Gallipoli. He wrote that the expedition was 'beastly ill-prepared, with no knowledge of where it is going, or what it would meet, or what it was going to do'. Lawrence was one of many officers who scoured Cairo bookshops looking for maps for the expedition while also trying to assemble some assessment of Turkish forces on the Gallipoli Peninsula. Several of his fellow officers also volunteered to serve with the expedition's intelligence staff. Lawrence was not allowed to go because his lack of experience in the field. At the same time he was involved in the preparation of plans to mount an expedition to Alexandretta (modern-day Iskenderun) on the Syrian coast. This plan had much to recommend it and could have served to out-flank Turkish forces in Syria by landing an army in its rear. To Lawrence's regret, this plan was eventually dropped as resources were allocated to the disastrous Gallipoli operation.

Lawrence's most important mission during this period came in March 1916 when he was sent to Mesopotamia, tasked with a number of assignments for both GHQ and the recently established Arab Bureau. Firstly, he was to meet with two defectors from the Ottoman Army: Major Aziz Ali al-Mazri and Captain Muhammad al-Faruqi. He was to assess their accounts of widespread discontent among Arab troops and gauge their suitability for leading any such rebellion. Secondly, Lawrence was to meet with Colonel Percy Cox, the chief political officer of the Indian Army forces in Mesopotamia, to explain to him the policies and functions of the Arab Bureau. Thirdly, he was to meet with the intelligence officers of this force in order to find areas of possible cooperation in the event of a revolt by the Arabs.

This mission resulted in a series of rather tense meetings with Indian Army officers, who resented his presence and the existence and aspirations of the Arab Bureau. Lawrence's discussions with both al-Mazri and al-Faruqi were also difficult. Both briefed Lawrence on an underground movement named al Ahd (the Covenant). They claimed that Arab forces were ready to rebel, and they sought British support and eventual independence in the event of this rebellion taking place. It would seem that their claims were somewhat exaggerated and Lawrence was also disappointed to learn that they were equally willing to entertain the possibility of support from Germany!

The inconclusive nature of the political aspects of Lawrence's mission was overshadowed by events at Kut. The local Ottoman commander, Khalil

Pasha, had suggested surrender terms to General Townshend. Townshend had responded by offering a cash payment if his army was allowed to leave Kut. This resulted in political pressure to see if al-Mazri and al-Faruqi could produce their promised rebellion, a solution abhorrent to the local commander, General Lake, who probably also correctly surmised that the plan was over-ambitious.

In the weeks that followed the situation grew increasingly bizarre. A cash offer of £1 million in gold was offered for the release of Townshend's army at Kut. In a secret communication, Cemal Pasha, the Ottoman governor of Syria and commander of 4th Field Army, asked if he would be recognized if he declared himself to be the independent ruler of Syria. Having met with Cox and Gertrude Bell, the noted expert on Iraqi affairs, Lawrence left Basra on 9 April 1916, bound for the front lines. Once there he found himself involved in one of the most surreal events of the war.

Lawrence arrived at General Lake's headquarters on 19 April, having travelled upriver on a gunboat. He received a frosty reception, as Lake viewed the attempt to incite rebellion as being totally dishonourable. Lawrence busied himself interrogating Arab POWs, but when another relieving force was defeated and an attempt to relieve Kut by river failed, the plan to buy the besieged army's release was resurrected. On the morning of 27 April Townshend renewed the offer of £1 million if Khalil Pasha allowed his men and artillery to leave Kut. After some deliberations by Khalil, the offer was turned down.

On 28 April Lawrence, together with two other officers (Herbert and Beach), was ordered to cross into Turkish lines and open fresh negotiations. They were empowered to offer an exchange of Arab POWs in return for the release of the sick and wounded at Kut. Crossing into no man's land under a flag of truce, Lawrence and his fellow officers were brought before Khalil Pasha, where they engaged in further unsuccessful talks. Lawrence used this as an opportunity to assess Khalil, and noted that the Ottoman commander was so unconvinced of the worth of Arab troops that he would not entertain the exchange. Lawrence chose to interpret this as being because of the growing discontent among Arab regiments. The party returned to British lines on the morning of 30 April. They had been treated well by their Turkish hosts, who had held a lavish dinner in their honour, but their mission was not a success.

Lawrence returned to Cairo totally disheartened. He was displeased with the result of the whole expedition. The Indian Army officers had been a profound disappointment and he was staggered by the ineptness of their campaign. At the same time he had been unsettled by the uncertain nature of their potential Arab allies. His report on this mission had to be toned down before final circulation because of the highly critical nature of his assessment. Events would soon take a critical turn that would open up a new and potentially decisive phase in the Middle Eastern theatre of operations, and Lawrence would find himself playing the role that he had long wished for.

THE HOUR OF DESTINY

Lawrence had shown himself to be a potentially difficult subordinate since his arrival in Cairo in 1914. Often bored and frustrated with military routine, this frustration could often boil over into veritable insubordination towards his superiors. This aspect of his character came increasingly to the fore after his return from Mesopotamia. In June, Major G. V. W. Holdich was appointed to command Section 1a. The two men had previously worked well together but soon the relationship began to break down as Lawrence became increasingly restless and critical. He took to correcting the punctuation and grammar in superiors' reports and became generally insufferable. The reason behind all this was simple – he was wangling for a posting to the Hejaz, in modern-day Saudi Arabia, where the Arab Revolt had finally broken out in June 1916. He was convinced that he had a vital role to play but was instead confined to a life of routine in Cairo. By the time Lawrence reached the Hejaz the revolt had been going on for several months, as he had been passed over in favour of officers with greater field experience.

Despite the fact that overtures had been made by the Arab leaders to GHQ in Cairo as early as April 1914, the outbreak of the revolt had come as a surprise. In the early months of 1916 it became increasingly apparent to Sharif Hussein of Mecca that the Ottoman authorities were about to move against him. Rumours had reached him that an alternative Sharif of Mecca (Sharif Ali Haidar of the rival Zaid branch of the Prophet Muhammed's descendents) was being considered. The Ottoman authorities also made an effort to control the importation of weapons and military *matériel* into the Hejaz, and Syrian nationalists informed Hussein that an expeditionary force was being formed in Damascus to move on Mecca.

Emir Feisal, the third son of Sharif Hussein. Lawrence quickly indentified that he was an inspirational leader. Also, Feisal's personal ambition led him to look towards Palestine and Syria as the location of a possible future kingdom for himself. (IWM Q58877)

Deciding that the time had come to rebel, Sharif Hussein entrusted field command to his sons. The size of the initial Arab Army is uncertain, but some estimates put it as large as 30,000 tribesmen. These were divided into smaller contingents commanded by the Emirs Ali, Abdullah, Feisal and Zeid. The initial contingents of tribesmen came from tribes whose tribal areas lay on the western coast of the Arabian Peninsula.

On 5 June 1916 the Emirs Ali and Feisal informed the Ottoman commander at Medina, General Fakhri Pasha, of Arab intentions to withdraw from the Ottoman Empire. Their subsequent attack on the town was repulsed and attacks on the Hejaz Railway followed, while telegraph lines were also cut. Five days later their father proclaimed the revolt in Mecca, and attacks were carried out on the garrisons there and at Ta'if. Despite the suddenness of the outbreak of revolt, the local Ottoman commanders at Ta'if and Mecca had obviously been expecting some form of attack. Under siege in buildings in both towns, the remaining Turkish troops continued to fight for several weeks.

At this critical juncture it was realized that outside help was necessary if the revolt was to continue. The port town of Jiddah was captured on 16 June with the aid of seaplanes from the Royal Navy's Red Sea Patrol, a naval flotilla that was to play a crucial role in the early months of the revolt. The seizure of this coastal town allowed for the landing of a party of British officers, Egyptian Army troops, mountain guns and machine guns on 30 June. This small force also brought money, food, weapons and over a million rounds of small-arms ammunition. Though the port towns of Yanbu and Rabegh were also captured in July, the remnants of the garrisons at Mecca and Ta'if held out, and it remained unclear if the Arab Revolt would be able to break out from the coastal area under its direct control. With support from Egyptian Army artillery, the last of the Mecca garrison was forced to surrender on 9 July, while the Ta'if garrison held on until 22 September before being finally being forced into submission. Sharif Hussein proclaimed himself to be 'king of the Arabs', a title that he was later encouraged by British officials to change to 'king of the Hejaz'.

During these first crucial weeks, Lawrence languished in Cairo, chafing at his inactivity. He compiled reports and projections on events in the Hejaz and liaised with the members of the Arab Bureau. He even designed a new set of stamps destined for use in the Hashemite kingdom of the Hejaz. But what he really wanted was to be sent into the field. As events unfolded in Arabia it was felt by many that the future of the revolt was uncertain. General Murray was urged to send a brigade to support the Arab forces, a move that he was reluctant to sanction as he wished to retain as many troops as possible in Egypt, and he was also sensitive to the possible consequences of sending European troops to campaign in a region that represented holy land for Muslims. A series of crucial meetings followed in September and October as senior officers in Cairo and officials from the Arab Bureau debated how the revolt could be nurtured or, indeed, if this was practical at all. Prominent in these debates were Colonel Cyril Wilson,

A locomotive of the Hejaz Railway. Lawrence identified this as being the main line of communication to Arabia. From 1917, Lawrence and other officers carried out a series of raids on the line in an effort to interrupt the flow of Turkish reinforcements and supplies. (IWM Q59650)

Sir Reginald Wingate and Sir Ronald Storrs. The general tone of these discussions was pessimistic as to the future of the Arabs' cause.

Another factor that had to be taken into account was the arrival of the French 'Military Mission to Egypt' in September 1916. As the French government had designs on Ottoman territory, it was made abundantly clear that the French considered this an Allied mission. The French force was based at Port Said and would eventually number over 1,100 men. It was initially commanded by Colonel Edouard Brémond, an experienced officer who had taken part in campaigns in French North Africa before the war. The French were also at a considerable advantage as they had Muslim officers and troops that they could deploy to Arabia almost immediately. Throughout the campaign Lawrence would endeavour to thwart French plans for the future of Arabia.

It was also known that Ottoman forces were preparing for a major offensive to put down the revolt. The key figure in Ottoman counter-moves was General Fakhri Pasha, whose army at Medina had been reinforced and who had also taken delivery of two new aircraft. In the autumn months of 1916 it seemed as though the revolt would be snuffed out before Christmas, as Arab troops and leaders were increasingly inactive while the senior commanders in Cairo debated whether or not their cause was worth further support. This inactivity would give Lawrence the chance he craved for.

In early October 1916 Colonel Clayton of Military Intelligence suggested that Lawrence be sent to Arabia to carry out an appraisal of the military situation and report back. While reports were already coming in from other British officers in the field, these were often contradictory, and, as Lawrence James has noted, these reports 'confused rather than enlightened'. Lawrence was being sent as a fresh pair of eyes. On 13 October 1916 he left Egypt on board the streamer *Lama* in company with Ronald Storrs of the Arab Bureau and Major al-Mazri, whom Lawrence had already met in Mesopotamia. Al-Mazri was a former officer of the Ottoman Army and, having spent time recruiting Arab POWs into the Arabian Army from among the ever-growing population of Ottoman prisoners in Egypt, was now being sent to Arabia to serve as Sharif Hussein's chief of staff. During the course of the two-day voyage, Lawrence discussed both the political and military future of the revolt. It is now known that al-Mazri proposed a military plan that was very similar to the one later adopted by Lawrence during his own campaign. Mazri's idea entailed the creation of a mobile flying column, which would include light artillery and would focus its efforts against the Hejaz Railway. The party arrived at Jiddah on 15 October 1916.

As was the case with his previous mission to Mesopotamia, Lawrence's assignment was multi-faceted. He was to converse with al-Mazri to discover his abilities, ambitions and plans. He was to assess the capabilities of the Arab Army and its leaders while also drawing up a clear picture of Ottoman forces and their dispositions. If he received permission to travel inland from Hussein he was to make contact with Feisal and his army, as it was felt that these were likely to face the brunt of the expected Ottoman counter-offensive. Lawrence was also to try to begin building up a new network of agents for military intelligence, as the agents then working for Hussein and his sons were thought to be totally unreliable. Finally, Lawrence was also to assess the officers of the British contingent, in particular Colonel Wilson, who, it was felt, was showing the strain of his difficult assignment.

Rabegh to Wejh, October 1916 to January 1917

Lawrence's initial role was, therefore, largely political. There were already a number of military officers with the Arab Army operating in a purely military role. These included Colonel Wilson, Lieutenant-Colonel Joyce and more junior officers such as Lieutenant (later Major) Garland. These officers, mostly on assignment from the Egyptian Army, busied themselves with the defence of the coastal towns and also the training of the Arab tribesmen. The Royal Navy's Red Sea Patrol, which included a seaplane carrier, was under the command of Captain Boyle, while a small Royal Flying Corps contingent was commanded by Captain A. J. Ross. Perhaps unsurprisingly, Lawrence succeeded in rubbing many of these officers up the wrong way with his opinionated style. By 22 October he had antagonized many, and Colonel Wilson cabled Colonel Clayton in Cairo stating that 'Lawrence wants kicking and kicking hard at that'. Wilson continued: 'I look on him as a bumptious young ass who spoils his undoubted knowledge of Syrian Arabs &c. by making himself out to be the only authority on war, engineering, HM's ships and everything else. He put every single person's back up I've met from the Admiral [Wemyss] down to the most junior fellow on the Red Sea.'

Where Lawrence came into his own was in dealing with the Arab leaders. He very quickly assessed the qualities of Hussein's elder sons (Ali and Abdullah) and realized that they intended to keep their forces in the proximity of Mecca and Medina. For long-term strategic goals they wished to concentrate Hashemite forces there as it was felt that by holding the two holiest towns in Islam they would ensure later Hashemite influence. In the late months of 1916 Lawrence's attention began to focus on Feisal, who was encamped near Yanbu with a force of around 8,000 tribesmen and 1,500 Egyptian troops and irregulars. Travelling across the desert, he first met Feisal near Hamra on 23 October 1916. He found the Arab leader depressed by recent military reverses and also hostile because of the fact that the British were supplying his army with weapons too slowly for his liking and were currently refusing to provide artillery.

It was at this initial meeting that Lawrence later claimed that Feisal asked him, 'How do you like our place here in Wadi Safra?', to which Lawrence replied, 'Well, but it is far from Damascus.' Whether or not this exchange actually took place at this time, it is interesting to note that in the months that followed Lawrence's and Feisal's gaze would

Lawrence frequently returned to Cairo to discuss the development of the Arab Revolt with senior intelligence and Arab Bureau officials at GHQ. He is photographed here with Commander David Hogarth and Colonel Alan Dawnay in March 1918. Hogarth was a former keeper at the Ashmolean Museum in Oxford and was head of the Arab Bureau from 1916. Dawnay coordinated the campaigns of the Arab Northern Army during 1918. (IWM Q59595)

indeed turn increasingly to the north-east. Feisal, as Hussein's third son, had little to expect from any post-war allocation of territories then held by the Ottomans in Arabia. He realized that he must look elsewhere, and this was an ambition encouraged by Lawrence, who saw that this facilitated wider British strategic goals.

In the short term, Feisal's main concern was the Turkish forces at Medina under Fakhri Pasha. In the final months of 1916 it was clear that forces were being massed in preparation for a counter-move against the Arabs. Initial encounters had not gone well for the Arabs, and it seemed likely that Turkish forces would push westwards in an attempt to recapture the port towns then in Arab hands. It was unlikely that the small number of British officers and Egyptian troops assigned to the Arab Army would be able to sway the outcome in the Arabs' favour.

Having promised Feisal further support, Lawrence returned to Cairo to report his assessment of the Arab leaders, emphasizing the usefulness of Feisal and his inspirational qualities as the leader of the Arab tribal forces. He also became embroiled in the debate as to whether a full British brigade should be sent to bolster the Arab forces. He correctly assessed that the majority of the Arab forces had neither the mindset, the training nor the weapons to mount a successful long-term defence of Rabegh and Yanbu, and he urged further support. It is clear, however, that at this time Lawrence felt that his role in the field was over and that he had returned to his proper place at GHQ in Cairo. On being told that he was to return to act as liaison officer to Feisal, he initially resisted, but sailed once more for Arabia on 25 November 1916.

He arrived just as the Arab Revolt faced its worst crisis. Fakhri Pasha had left Medina with a force of around two brigades, intent on recapturing Yanbu and then Rabegh. Turkish forces had outflanked an Arab position in Wadi Safra on 1 December and the Arab forces had broken and fled. Then an Arab force at Hamra under Emir Zeid had also been defeated, leaving the Ottoman commander in control of the routes to both Yanbu and Rabegh. Lawrence

Command meeting with Emir Feisal, Hamra, October 1916

Lawrence had been sent to Arabia in October 1916 to assess the progress of the revolt and to report on the potential of the Arab leaders. He first met Emir Feisal on 23 October 1916 at a time when the revolt had stalled and Feisal himself had suffered a series of reverses and been pushed back by the Turks to Hamra. In a series of meetings, Lawrence (at that time a very junior officer) and Feisal discussed future plans for the revolt. In the initial meeting, Lawrence found Feisal quite hostile because of the small number of arms that had been provided by the British and also the lack of artillery. It was ultimately decided that it was essential that the Arab Army hold the coastal towns of Yanbu and Rabegh. This would facilitate supply by sea and also evacuation if necessary. During the actions that followed between December 1916 and January 1917, the support of the Royal Navy's Red Sea Patrol would prove to be decisive. Lawrence (1) is shown here with Arab headdress but otherwise in uniform. Feisal (2) is assisted by his secretary (3) while in the background stands a heavily armed bodyguard (4).

Since the beginning of the Arab Revolt, airpower had proved very effective. At different times aircraft of the Royal Naval Air Service and the RFC/RAF had cooperated with Arab forces. Here Lieutenant Murphy shows his Bristol F2 fighter to an Arab tribesman. (IWM Q58702)

found Feisal at Nakhl Mubarak on 2 December with a force of around 4,000 tribesmen. Despite the desperate situation, Lawrence found Feisal calm and dignified. In the days that followed, the fortunes of the Arab Revolt hung in the balance as Turkish forces, moving gradually towards Yanbu, pushed aside the Arab forces sent to oppose them. Lawrence laid out a forward airfield for use by the RFC flight based at Yanbu. It was at this time, Lawrence later claimed, that Feisal invited him to wear Arab dress and presented him with a set of robes that he had had sent from Mecca. Whatever the truth of this claim, he would wear Arab robes while in the field from that point on.

After further hurried meetings with the Arab leaders, Lawrence hastened back to Yanbu where he found Lt. Garland busy preparing the defence of the town with a force of around 1,500 men. Lawrence sent an urgent message to Captain Boyle of the Royal Navy's Red Sea Patrol, and ultimately it would be Royal Naval support that would turn the balance in the Arabs' favour. Five ships of the Red Sea Patrol arrived off the coast at Yanbu, including a monitor, *M.31*, which was capable of moving close inshore to provide fire support. The small flotilla also included the *Raven*, a seaplane carrier, and in the days that followed Royal Navy seaplanes attacked the Turkish columns as they advanced on the town. When Arab forces at Nakhl Mubarak were driven back on 9 December, the route to the town lay open. The turning point came during the night of 11–12 December when the Turks had advanced right to Yanbu, but they called off their attack because Fakhri Pasha realized that Royal Navy guns and searchlights covered the town. Even still, he proceeded with his advance southwards towards Rabegh and continued this operation until 18 January when, faced with logistical problems, RFC attacks on Medina, sickness in his army and attacks along his lines of communication, the Ottoman commander called off his offensive. It had been a close-run thing, and this series of reverses had almost seen the Arab Revolt snuffed out while still in its infancy.

A crucial factor in the Turkish decision to cease operations at this point was the news that the Royal Navy and the Arab Army were moving on Wejh, the last Ottoman-held port in the Hejaz. This scheme had been mooted before but was revived by Colonel Wilson in December 1916. Such a move would facilitate later attacks on the Hejaz Railway. In an immediate sense, it would deflect Turkish forces from Rabegh. In a wider strategic sense, it would force the Turks to expend manpower in protecting the railway line, which extended for over 1,300km (800 miles) to Damascus. Using a supply of British gold, Feisal assembled a large tribal force from among the Agayl, Juhayna, 'Utayba,

Harb and Billi tribes. When finally assembled this force numbered over 8,000 tribesmen, and Arab leaders acknowledged that it was the largest tribal army in living memory. Lawrence travelled in the first section of this large column, alongside Feisal and his Agayl bodyguard, embarking on an expedition to Wejh, over 320km (200 miles) away.

The plan to take Wejh was relatively simple. A Royal Navy force, including *Fox*, *Hardinge* and *Espiegle*, commanded by Admiral Wemyss, would move in close to the shore and

Photograph taken by Lawrence of the Arab Army on the march towards Wejh in January 1917. Emir Feisal is in white robes in front of his standard bearers. (IWM Q58863)

support the Arab Army that would attack from the landward side. On board these Royal Navy ships were around 600 Arab volunteers, who would undertake a landing at the same time. However, when Wemyss arrived off the town on 23 January 1917, he found no trace of the Arab Army. The town was defended by around 800 men of the Turkish 129th Infantry Battalion and a levy of 500 tribesmen of the Agayl. Moreover, the town's population was known to be anti-Hashemite, so there was a risk that they would join in the defence. Nevertheless, Wemyss decided that he must go ahead with the assault, as time was of the essence and he felt that the Arab force on board his ships could achieve the objective if supported by naval gunfire, naval landing parties and seaplanes.

The fight to take Wejh lasted throughout the day as Arab forces and Royal Navy personnel engaged in a street-by-street battle for the town. It was not until the next morning that the final Ottoman troops in the town surrendered. Around 20 Arabs and one RFC officer had been killed in the assault, with many wounded. The supporting attack from Feisal's army never occurred. Feisal, Lawrence and the Arab Army did not show up at Wejh until 25 January.

In the days that followed, there was much recrimination between the British officers, Feisal and Lawrence. Lawrence chided the Royal Navy officers for their impatience and made the valid point that moving such a large tribal army over such a distance presented difficulties and made it difficult to reach Wejh on schedule. Despite his defence of Arab tardiness, Lawrence realized that the failure to show up on time at Wejh cast doubt on their worth as a fighting force and that it would make his efforts to support them more difficult in the future. He was correct in stating that Feisal's main achievement lay in the actual creation of the army. It now stood in close proximity to the main Ottoman supply line: the Hejaz Railway. As such it presented a major threat to Ottoman power in Arabia. Over the months that followed, Lawrence and other British officers would turn this threat into reality as they embarked upon a concerted campaign against the Hejaz Railway.

Captain Wood, Trooper Thorne and T. E. Lawrence prepare to embark on an expedition against the Hejaz Railway. Lawrence appears to be loading a Colt .45 automatic, a weapon he later confessed to finding extremely effective. (IWM Q60099)

The railway campaign, 1917

The march to Wejh in early 1917 marked a crucial juncture in the history of the Arab Revolt. Following the setbacks of late 1916, the initiative passed once again to the Arabs. This signalled to other tribes that the revolt would continue, and, equally important, that it would continue to be backed by both the British and the French. On their arrival in Wejh, Feisal had asked that Lawrence be seconded to his army, and this new assignment was sanctioned by GHQ in Cairo. What had begun as yet another temporary assignment for Lawrence was now of open-ended duration, and, despite his earlier misgivings about returning to the field, he seems to have relished this new assignment from the beginning. Lawrence noted that during the weeks that followed, tribal leaders from the Shararat, the Bani 'Atiya, the Billi and the Howeitat came to Wejh to pledge their allegiance to Feisal and the Hashemite cause. Of even more interest to Lawrence was the fact that some tribal leaders arrived from as far away as Ottoman Syria, signalling to him the possibilities of fomenting revolt in that region. On occasion, however, tribal animosities boiled over into virtual mutiny, and these difficult situations had to be defused by Feisal.

In the wider strategic perspective, the move to Wejh was well timed as it facilitated a major effort against the Hejaz Railway. Lawrence's and Feisal's initial plan was to attack the railway and interdict supplies and reinforcements heading to Medina. In the best-case scenario, the large Turkish garrison there of over 12,000 men would eventually be forced to surrender. These attacks would also force the Turks to dissipate their forces along the railway line in order to defend it. By March 1917 the emphasis on this campaign changed. Intelligence staff in Cairo had learned that Fakhri Pasha had been ordered to evacuate Medina. Fakhri Pasha had successfully protested these orders, but this was unknown at GHQ and it was ordered that the attacks on the railway should increase, as it was essential to hold Fakhri Pasha in Medina. The movement of the Turkish garrison at this time would have resulted in a stiffening of Turkish defences in Palestine, where a new offensive was soon to be launched. This offensive, led by General Murray (the first battle of Gaza), began on 26 March 1917, and, although it was a failure, it set in motion a concerted campaign against the Hejaz Railway that would continue for the rest of the war.

Throughout the early months of 1917 small parties had left Wejh and headed out to the railway. These were commanded by Lieutenant-Colonel Stewart Newcombe, Lt. Henry Garland and Lieutenant Hornby, together with Arab officers such as Major al-Mazri, who was an early advocate of the railway campaign. The absence of these officers often left Lawrence in command at Wejh as the senior British officer. His lack of field experience ensured that he was not an obvious choice for the initial raids, but this would later change.

Still primarily concerned with political duties, in March 1917 he undertook a long desert journey to Wadi 'Ais in order to pass on instructions to Emir Abdullah. Having contacted Emir Abdullah, who was to keep his army in the vicinity of Medina to harass the garrison and attack the railway, Lawrence carried on eastwards until they reached the railway between Aba al-Na'am and Istabl Antar. While he had focused so much of his attention on the railway over the preceding months, this was actually the first time that he had seen it. Lawrence and his party cut the line in two places, cut the telegraph line and also laid mines, one of which partly derailed an approaching train. While they were eventually driven off by Turkish fire, Lawrence's first raid had been a success and, as was characteristic with him, he factored in the lessons he had learned for future operations.

Above: Not a wartime demolition! The special-effects crew of David Lean's *Lawrence of Arabia* prepare to mine a train for one of the film's most dramatic scenes. (Author's Collection)

During the months that followed, Lawrence and other officers led numerous raids against the Hejaz Railway – far too numerous for them all to be dealt with here. In the initial stages the raiding parties were quite small, consisting of perhaps just a dozen men. As the campaign progressed they increased in size and sometimes numbered up to 200 men. Different methods were used to cause a maximum amount of damage. Lawrence and his colleagues quickly realized that rather than blowing up sections of rail, it was better to bend the rails out of shape with 'tulip mines', so called because they bent the metal rails into shapes not unlike tulip bulbs. This ensured that Turkish repair parties first had to dismantle the sections of damaged line before replacing them. This increased the work; replacing line that had simply been blown away took half the time. Lawrence also preferred to damage curved sections of the line as, once again, it was more difficult to source and fit new rails for these sections.

Below: A wartime photograph of a mine exploding on the Hejaz Railway. This appears to be a 'tulip mine', which were designed to bend the rails out of shape in order to make it more difficult for repair parties. Some of the raids on the line entailed the detonation of dozens of charges. (IWM Q60020)

Apart from the actual railway, Lawrence and his raiding parties also began to target ancillary infrastructure. The telegraph line running beside the railway was an obvious target. They attacked and damaged station buildings, paying particular attention to water towers. They fired upon the Turkish blockhouses defending the line and made bridges a particular target. On one particular occasion, a raiding party under Lawrence

and Lt. Col. Joyce demolished either end of a bridge but left the seriously damaged centre section standing. This ensured that the repair party first had to undertake a dangerous demolition before rebuilding the bridge. The ultimate prize was, perhaps inevitably, to derail a moving train, a feat first carried out by Lt. Garland in February 1917.

These attacks achieved their desired effect and seriously interrupted the flow of supplies to Medina. It also made it virtually impossible to evacuate that city, had Fakhri Pasha wanted to. For the rest of the war the Turkish Army had to expend manpower in protecting the railway and also in organizing mobile columns to counter the raiding parties. However, the ultimate effectiveness of the railway campaign is still a subject of debate. In an interview with Lt. Henry Garland after the war, Fakhri Pasha claimed that the Medina garrison had never been near starvation, as they were still supplied by the pro-Ottoman Shammar tribe. While the railway demolitions were a great annoyance, he still maintained an army of over 10,000 effectives at the end of the war, and the Medina garrison did not actually surrender until January 1919!

Aqaba, May–July 1917

If one was to single out just one episode of Lawrence's career in Arabia for praise, it would have to be his epic march on Aqaba in the summer of 1917. In a period of over two months he led a small group of tribesmen through inhospitable enemy territory in order to carry out a *coup de main* attack on a strategically important town. While the action itself was impressive, Lawrence's timing was also excellent as the momentum of the revolt had somewhat dissipated.

By May 1917 the Arab forces had essentially evolved into three armies. The Arab Northern Army under Feisal was based at Wejh. Further south, the Arab Southern Army commanded by Emir Ali was located near Medina, while the Arab Eastern Army, under Emir Abdullah, was to the east of Mecca. The armies of Emirs Ali and Abdullah would essentially remain in these locations for the

Aqaba on the Red Sea coast. Lawrence and Feisal recognized that the seizure of this port town would later allow them to take the Arab Northern Army towards Palestine, Lebanon and Syria. (IWM Q59548)

rest of war in order to counter the Ottoman forces at Medina and the Shammar tribesmen of the interior.

While the campaign against the Hejaz Railway was proving to be a success for Feisal and Lawrence, they sought ways to further prosecute the war. Lawrence noted how some tribesmen were drifting away to return to their homelands. At the same time, Syrian tribesmen were arriving at Wejh, urging Feisal to carry the revolt to their tribal homelands and promising support. Prominent among these were Auda abu Tayi, leader of the warlike Howeitat tribe, and also the Syrian leaders Nasib al-Bakri and Zaki Drubi. The aspirations of these Arab leaders fitted neatly with those of both Feisal and Lawrence. Feisal recognized that the fertile regions of Palestine and Syria would facilitate the survival of a future Hashemite state in the Hejaz.

Also, by May 1917, the details of the Sykes-Picot Agreement had reached Arabia. This agreement, ratified by Britain, France and Russia in May 1916, would divide up Ottoman territory in Arabia and the Levant among the Allied powers after the war. Lawrence wished to thwart French designs on Syria by helping to create an existing Arab state ruled by Feisal. It is certain that these secret arrangements disgusted him. For the remainder of the war Lawrence had to try to keep the Arabs on the Allies' side while at the same time knowing that their aspirations for independence would not be realized. In a letter to Clayton (now a brigadier-general) written in June 1917, the strain this duplicity put on Lawrence is apparent, even to the extent of a suggestion of suicide: 'Clayton. I've decided to go off alone to Damascus, hoping to get killed on the way: for all sakes try and clear up this show before it goes further. We are calling them to fight for us on a lie, and I can't stand it.'

In this heated political context Lawrence's attention fixed on Aqaba, the last Red Sea port still in Ottoman hands. Deemed to be too well defended for a naval assault and landing, Lawrence realized that if it could be seized it could serve as a base for the advance of Feisal's army towards Palestine, Lebanon and Syria. It also served a wider strategic purpose, as seizure of Aqaba would further isolate Medina, while allowing for further attacks on the northern sections of the Hejaz Railway. An Arab Army based there would also keep Ottoman forces in the Sinai and Palestine off-balance as they prepared to defend against further British offensives.

Lawrence initially presented this plan as a long-range raid with Ma'an as its objective, timed to coincide with a major raid being carried out by Newcombe in the direction of al 'Ula. On 9 May 1917 Lawrence left Wejh with a small party including Sharif Nasir, Auda and Za'al Abu Tayi, Nasib al-Bakri, Zaki Drubi and Mohammed adh-Dhaylan. A group of 17 Agayl tribesmen also

Lawrence photographed in 1917 with Auda abu Tayi, the hereditary war chief of the Howeitat tribe. Auda was a born guerrilla leader and in 1917 Lawrence undertook an expedition with him to capture the strategic port town of Aqaba. (IWM Q60102)

Arab tribesmen attacking Aqaba on 6 July 1917. This has become one of the most iconic images of the campaign and was taken by Lawrence himself. (IWM Q59193)

travelled with him, under the command of Ibn Dgaythir. The plan was to make contact with the Howeitat near Aqaba and enlist them for the attack on the town. To this end, Lawrence's party carried over £20,000 in gold coin for the purposes of paying the Howeitat tribesmen.

Lawrence, who had grown more accustomed to life in the desert, nevertheless found the weeks that followed particularly gruelling. The plan was to carry a wide sweeping approach to the north-east of Aqaba, attacking the town by advancing through Wadi Ithm. To do this they had to cover over 1,000km (620 miles) of desert. One section was so feared among Arabs as to be known as 'al-Houl', or 'the Terror'. On crossing the Hejaz Railway on 19 May, Lawrence carried out demolitions and cut the railway in the hope that the Turks would suspect that this was a mere raiding party. His fears were probably unfounded, as such an approach to Aqaba would have seemed unimaginable to Turkish commanders.

It was during this section of the march that he searched for one of his servants, Gasim, who had fallen from his camel and was missing. It was a dangerous and perhaps foolhardy enterprise and his fellow travellers were less than sympathetic to Gasim's plight. Lawrence later described his return, having rescued the missing Gasim: 'Auda pointed to the wretched hunched up figure and denounced me. "For that thing, not worth a camel's price…" I interrupted him with "Not worth a half-crown, Auda", and he, delighted in his simple mind, rode near Gasim, and struck him sharply, trying to make him repeat, like a parrot, his price.'

Having recruited some friendly tribesmen en route, Lawrence left his party in Wadi Sirhan and continued northwards to meet with Syrian leaders. In a separate round trip of around 800km (500 miles) he ventured as far as the outskirts of Damascus, where he met with local leaders and convinced them not to begin their rebellion prematurely. During this expedition within a greater expedition he carried out a diversionary attack and demolished a bridge near Ras Baalbek, an attack that resulted in six Ottoman battalions being taken out of the line to counter what was feared to be the beginning of a general uprising. Throughout this expedition to Damascus Lawrence also carried out a reconnaissance, which he hoped would be of use to GHQ when planning further operations into Palestine and Syria.

On his return to Wadi Sirhan on 17 June he found that the Arab leaders had recruited 500 men of the Howeitat, 150 men of the Rwalla and the Shararat and 35 tribesmen from the Kawikiba. With this force, Lawrence began his last approach towards Aqaba. While the main Ottoman defences in the town were designed to defend against attack from the sea, there were

The capture of Aqaba, May–July 1917

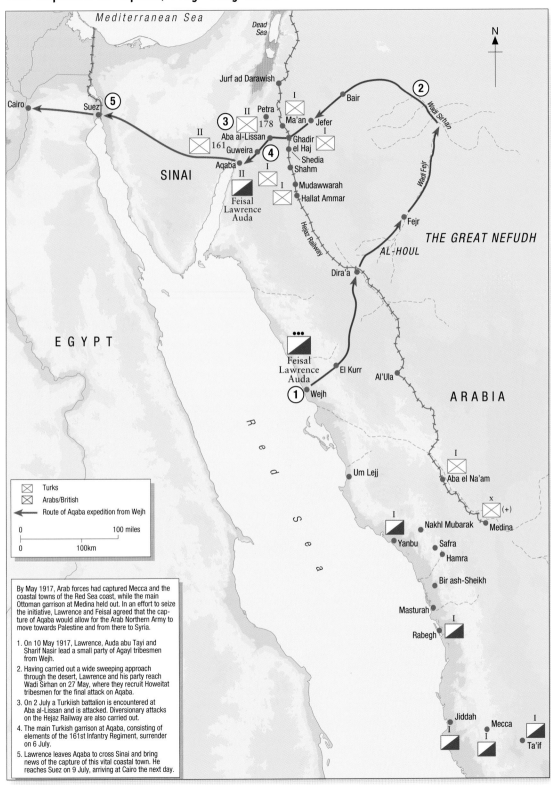

Turks

Arabs/British

Route of Aqaba expedition from Wejh

| 0 | | 100 miles |
| 0 | 100km | |

By May 1917, Arab forces had captured Mecca and the coastal towns of the Red Sea coast, while the main Ottoman garrison at Medina held out. In an effort to seize the initiative, Lawrence and Feisal agreed that the capture of Aqaba would allow for the Arab Northern Army to move towards Palestine and from there to Syria.

1. On 10 May 1917, Lawrence, Auda abu Tayi and Sharif Nasir lead a small party of Agayl tribesmen from Wejh.

2. Having carried out a wide sweeping approach through the desert, Lawrence and his party reach Wadi Sirhan on 27 May, where they recruit Howeitat tribesmen for the final attack on Aqaba.

3. On 2 July a Turkiish battalion is encountered at Aba al-Lissan and is attacked. Diversionary attacks on the Hejaz Railway are also carried out.

4. The main Turkish garrison at Aqaba, consisting of elements of the 161st Infantry Regiment, surrender on 6 July.

5. Lawrence leaves Aqaba to cross Sinai and bring news of the capture of this vital coastal town. He reaches Suez on 9 July, arriving at Cairo the next day.

also Ottoman troops between Lawrence's force and Aqaba. The Turks had also destroyed the wells to the north-east of the town, which suggests that they were alert to the possibility of some kind of attacking force emerging from the desert. Diversionary attacks were carried out against the railway and, around 30 June, a party of the Howeitat took the Ottoman fort at Fuweilah, killing almost the entire garrison in reprisal for recent Turkish treatment of the local population. This fort was eventually recaptured by elements of the 178th Regiment.

Lawrence then learned that the main contingent of this battalion was encamped at Aba al-Lissan, essentially barring his advance on Aqaba. On 2 July Lawrence and the Arab leaders decided to attack, having first positioned their tribal forces in the hills around Aba al-Lissan. Lawrence was unable to encourage the Arabs into a decisive assault on the Turkish battalion and the affair settled into a prolonged and desultory firefight. In the fierce heat of the afternoon the attack stalled completely as the tribesmen sought shelter from the sun. Lawrence was faced with a dilemma. The longer this attack stalled, the more likely it was that Turkish reinforcements would arrive. If his force was thwarted at this point, not only would they not take Aqaba, but they would face the impossible task of having to retreat back to Wejh. This was not a realistic option. In a carefully worded exchange with Auda abu Tayi he chided the tribesmen for their inactivity, and this had the desired result. Auda led a charge of around 50 horsemen into the Turkish battalion. The attack took the Turks off-balance and they lost their cohesion, suffering around 300 fatalities while 160 were taken prisoner.

Further small outlying garrisons were overrun during the days that followed. These included the Turkish positions at Guweira, Kathira and Hadra. One of the captured Turkish officers was persuaded to send letters

Lawrence at Aqaba in 1917, mounted on one of his racing camels. The capture of the town ensured his increasing prominence in the planning of the wider campaign. (IWM Q60212)

tothe garrison in Aqaba offering them assurances that they would be treated properly if they surrendered. Lawrence and his companions found further posts abandoned as they made their final march on the town. On 5 July there was a short exchange of fire at Khadra in the evening and as both sides settled down for the night. Lawrence found that his force had swelled to over 1,000 men as further tribesmen of the Howeitat and the Haywat arrived to take part in the final attack.

Attempts at negotiations to induce surrender tried Lawrence's nerves but, after an exchange of fire on the morning of 6 July, the Turkish commander at Aqaba decided to capitulate. No timely reinforcement from Ma'an seemed possible, and by coincidence a Royal Navy gunboat, the *Slieve Foy*, had arrived and had begun shelling the town. The Arabs' final dash took the own without a shot being fired. Lawrence later summed up the final act in his memoir of the war, *Seven Pillars of Wisdom*: 'Then we raced through a driving

Arab tribesmen assembled in Wadi Ithm, to the north of Aqaba, on 5 July 1917. Having carried out a gradual approach towards the town over a number of weeks, Lawrence and Auda Abu Tayi led a final assault on Aqaba on 6 July 1917. It is thought that Lawrence took this photo during the final day before the assault. (IWM Q59207)

sand-storm down to Aqaba four miles further, and splashed into the sea on July the sixth, just two months after our setting out from Wejh.'

It had indeed been an audacious expedition and Lawrence would attempt another wide sweeping approach when attempting to blow a bridge in the Yarmuk Valley later in the year. He was equally impressed with the growing confidence of the Arab tribesmen when confronting regular Turkish forces. Above all, the capture of Aqaba would allow Feisal's Arab Northern Army to be moved up the coast. In the months that followed their very presence at Aqaba would pose a threat to Turkish forces in Arabia, with the isolation of the Medina garrison a real possibility. Also, Lawrence knew that further operations were planned into Palestine and that the Arab Revolt could play an important part in them by tying down the Turkish left. It was one of the most unqualified successes of the war and acted as inspiration for later desert operations during World War II.

Lawrence set out on 7 July and crossed Sinai in order to reach Suez and from there to Cairo, which he reached on 10 July. He found that Murray had been replaced by General Sir Edmund Allenby, who immediately appreciated the significance of the capture of Aqaba and the potential of the Arab Revolt. Lawrence secured promises of further support, and this steady supply of weapons, personnel and larger equipment, such as Rolls-Royce armoured cars, would see the potential of the Arab Revolt realized.

Guerrilla war, 1917–18

Lawrence realized that the capture of Aqaba opened a new series of strategic possibilities. To the north-east lay a route starting in Wadi Ithm that could eventually be used to advance into Palestine and Syria. Also, with Aqaba used as a base for the Arab Northern Army, they could now operate more effectively against the Hejaz Railway. The vital stations at Ma'an and Mudawarrah were now brought within striking distance and were to become objectives for the Arab Army in late 1917 and 1918, albeit tough ones to crack because of the size of the Ottoman garrisons there.

Jafar Pasha al-Askari, Emir Feisal and Lt. Col. Joyce drinking tea at Wadi Quntilla in August 1917. As the Arab Northern Army grew in size, its regular contingent was officered by former Ottoman officers such as Jafar Pasha. Joyce commanded 'Operation Hedgehog', the British mission to the Arab Northern Army. Lawrence found himself increasingly responsible for the irregular tribal contingent. (IWM Q59011)

In the weeks that followed the capture of Aqaba, the Arab Northern Army moved from Wejh to Aqaba, facilitated by the Royal Navy. Lawrence had been promoted to major and initially had hopes of becoming the senior British officer at Aqaba. Ultimately, Lt. Col. Joyce was placed in command, but Lawrence remained as the main liaison with Feisal and also as the senior British officer with the tribal contingents. This was the role he would essentially fill until the end of the war.

The Arab Northern Army had by now grown to include both a regular contingent and an irregular force of Arab tribesmen. The regular contingent was commanded by Jafar Pasha al-Askari. Along with other former Ottoman officers, he commanded a force of around 2,000 men, mostly ex-POWs, who were organized along conventional lines. The regular army was divided into two divisions, supported by a camel corps, an artillery battery, a machine-gun detachment and associated logistical and medical units. The irregular tribal force was essentially Lawrence's concern and at times this swelled to around 6,000 men from tribes such the Howeitat, the Bani 'Ali and the Juhaynah, amongst others. Tactical command rested with the leaders of each tribal contingent, while Lawrence and Feisal oversaw the general direction of their actions.

This considerable force was supported by Royal Navy gunboats anchored in Aqaba to provide fire support in the event of a Turkish counter-attack. To counter the activities of Turkish planes that attacked Aqaba on a daily basis from their base at Ma'an, air support was provided by a flight of the RFC. This small flight carried out reconnaissance work, attacked Turkish troops on the ground and regularly flew to Ma'an to carry out bombing raids. Backing all of this activity was a steady flow of funds from Cairo; each month thousands of pounds in gold coin were dispensed as wages to the Arab forces, and also to fund wider activities.

Yarmuk Valley Raid, November 1917

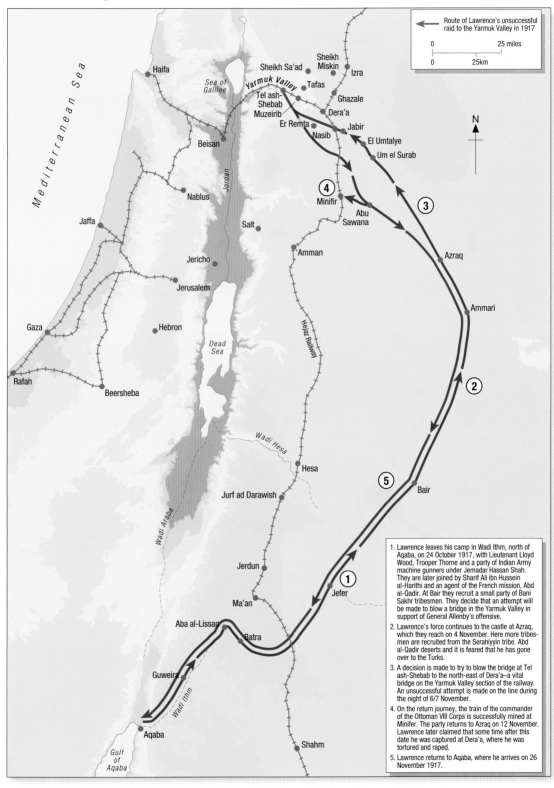

Route of Lawrence's unsuccessful raid to the Yarmuk Valley in 1917

0   25 miles

0   25km

N

Mediterranean Sea

Haifa

Sea of Galilee

Sheikh Miskin

Sheikh Sa'ad

Izra

Tafas

Yarmuk Valley

Ghazale

Tel ash-Shebab
Muzeirib

Dera'a

Er Remta

Jabir

Nasib

El Umtalye

Um el Surab

Beisan

Jordan

4

Minifir

Abu Sawana

Nablus

Jaffa

Salt

'Amman

Azraq

Jericho

3

Jerusalem

Hejaz Railway

Ammari

Gaza

Hebron

Dead Sea

2

Rafah

Beersheba

Wadi Hesa

Hesa

Jurf ad Darawish

5

Bair

Wadi Araba

Jerdun

1

Ma'an

Jefer

Aba al-Lissan

Batra

Guweira

Wadi Ithm

Aqaba

Shahm

Gulf of Aqaba

1. Lawrence leaves his camp in Wadi Ithm, north of Aqaba, on 24 October 1917, with Lieutenant Lloyd Wood, Trooper Thorne and a party of Indian Army machine gunners under Jemadar Hassan Shah. They are later joined by Sharif Ali ibn Hussein al-Harithi and an agent of the French mission, Abd al-Qadir. At Bair they recruit a small party of Bani Sakhr tribesmen. They decide that an attempt will be made to blow a bridge in the Yarmuk Valley in support of General Allenby's offensive.

2. Lawrence's force continues to the castle at Azraq, which they reach on 4 November. Here more tribesmen are recruited from the Serahiyyin tribe. Abd al-Qadir deserts and it is feared that he has gone over to the Turks.

3. A decision is made to try to blow the bridge at Tel ash-Shebab to the north-east of Dera'a–a vital bridge on the Yarmuk Valley section of the railway. An unsuccessful attempt is made on the line during the night of 6/7 November.

4. On the return journey, the train of the commander of the Ottoman VIII Corps is successfully mined at Minifer. The party returns to Azraq on 12 November. Lawrence later claimed that some time after this date he was captured at Dera'a, where he was tortured and raped.

5. Lawrence returns to Aqaba, where he arrives on 26 November 1917.

A Turkish work party repairing demolitions to the Hejaz Railway. Lawrence reportedly took this photograph himself. (IWM Q60116)

Despite the success of the Aqaba raid and the potential of the Arab Army gathering there, this was a difficult time for Lawrence, and once again the revolt fell into a period of inactivity. As further details of the Sykes-Picot Agreement leaked out, relations with the Hashemite leaders worsened, and as the Anglo-Arab relationship reached an all-time low Lawrence tried to limit the damage by interpreting the agreement in a more positive light to Feisal and, through him, Sharif Hussein. Intelligence that the Ottoman government was offering large sums in gold to the tribal leaders and even Hussein to end their revolt further added to Lawrence's political concerns. The possibility of a Turkish counter-move on Aqaba also loomed, and while a large force did venture out from Ma'an, this Turkish offensive petered out within a few months.

At the same time, military activity had to be sustained and raids on the Hejaz Railway continued. These had grown in size and audacity as the Arab Army grew and gained confidence in countering Turkish forces while out on raids. On one raid in July 1917 over 500 charges were detonated on the line south of al 'Ula. By this stage in the campaign the tactics employed during railway raids had also evolved, and Lawrence was one of the prime movers in this respect. He realized that when operating in the proximity of the larger railway garrisons his tribal forces could not be expected to engage them on an equal basis. An increased level of firepower within the raiding parties would, Lawrence felt, overcome this imbalance. Where possible, he would include machine-gun teams and mortar teams in his raiding parties. This tactical policy would later be expanded to include mountain guns, truck-mounted artillery and armoured cars. A typical example of Lawrence's use of firepower was his raid on Mudawwarah during the night of 17–18 September 1917. His original objective was the well, and he hoped to destroy this and leave a 240km (150-mile) section of the railway without a source of water. He took two British NCOs (Sergeant Yells and Corporal Brook) with him to operate a Lewis light

Apart from attacking Turkish forces, the aircraft attached to the Arab Northern Army carried out important reconnaissance work. This is a test aerial photo of the RFC base at Aqaba in 1917. (IWM Q105642)

machine gun and a Stokes mortar. Lawrence's force could not approach Mudawwarah station too closely because of the Turkish garrison of over 300 men there, but the light machine-gun and mortar teams kept them contained while Lawrence laid a large mine on a nearby bridge. This mine destroyed not only the bridge but also a train that had been passing over it. (Lawrence later noted that this train had carried both women and the sick.) Such tactics would be used on many future raids and allowed demolition teams to work while greater firepower kept the enemy suppressed.

Between 26 September and 1 October, Lawrence and Captain Pisani of the French mission led a party of 80 tribesmen on another railway raid. Apart from destroying sections of the railway and an important bridge, they also managed to destroy a train. The Arab regular army was also beginning to push into the south of the Sinai, and on 21 October it defeated a large Turkish force at Wadi Musa, near Petra. Lawrence, who had long been a believer in air power, wished to facilitate aircraft travelling from Suez over the Sinai, and as early as August 1917 had begun laying out temporary airfields in the Sinai. These were stocked with petrol and bombs and they later proved to be of considerable value to aircraft travelling on bombing raids to the Turkish left flank. In this hectic period between September and October 1917 Lawrence engaged in a series of continuous attacks on the railway, ranging as far as Kilometre 589, south of Ma'an. During this raid he destroyed a train but was also injured in the hip by a Turkish bullet. Lawrence also shared his newly acquired dynamiting knowledge with his tribal contingent. In the months that followed they dynamited 17 trains and caused much destruction along the railway.

On 11 October Lawrence flew to Cairo for a second meeting with General Allenby. Allenby was planning a new offensive on the Gaza–Beersheba line (the third battle of Gaza) that was scheduled to begin at the end of the month. Lawrence had previously promised that a general rebellion could be initiated in Syria, something that he no longer believed possible and realized would result in widespread reprisals among the Syrian population. Lawrence now proposed that he destroy the westernmost bridge in the Yarmuk Valley at Jisr al-Hemmi. This was an impressive steel bridge spanning a large gorge

Camel-mounted troops of the Indian Army crossing Sinai. During 1917 and 1918 Lawrence used Indian and Gurkha mortar and machine-gun teams to provide firepower for his tribal forces.
(IWM Q103859)

Azrak Castle near Amman. This former Crusader castle served as Lawrence's base for the Yarmuk Valley raid in November 1917. (IWM Q60022)

and, despite being a key piece of infrastructure, intelligence indicated that it was guarded by just a dozen sentries. Its destruction would stop railway traffic for at least two weeks and cut the main line of retreat for the Turks between Jerusalem and Damascus. It was hoped that the Syrian population would then rebel and attack Turkish forces as they retreated on foot. Lawrence agreed to try to blow this bridge on 5 November or on one of the three succeeding nights. It was a huge undertaking and, although Lawrence remained outwardly confident, his colleagues realized that the strain was getting to him. Clayton, the chief of intelligence, noted: 'I am very anxious about Lawrence. He has taken on a really colossal job and I can see that it is well-nigh weighing him down.'

During this important raid Lawrence essentially tried to repeat the same methods that had brought him success at Aqaba. He planned to carry out a wide sweeping approach, travelling north-eastwards before basing himself at the partly-ruined Crusader castle at Azrak. He would travel with just a small party of tribesmen, as not many could be persuaded to travel so far north, although he did later recruit men of the Bani Shakr and the Serahiyyin at Azrak. He was accompanied by an Indian Army machine-gun team under Jamadar Hassan Shah and by Lieutenant Wood (Royal Engineers) and Trooper Throne (Yeomanry). Attached to his group was Abd al-Qadir (also Abd el-Kader), an Algerian exile in Syria and grandson of a guerrilla leader who had carried out a long campaign against the French in the 19th century. The head of the French mission, Colonel Brémond, had warned Lawrence that he suspected al-Qadir of being a Turkish spy, of which Lawrence took no notice.

Attack on the Hejaz Railway, 1 January 1918

The allocation of a squadron of Rolls-Royce armoured cars, Talbot cars equipped with 10-pdr guns and light Ford cars provided the Arab Army with an increased level of mobile firepower. In late 1917 Lawrence and Lt. Col. Joyce experimented with these cars by travelling across country towards the Hejaz Railway. On 1 January 1918 they carried out a series of attacks on Turkish blockhouses north of the important railway station at Mudawwarah. The armoured plating of the Rolls-Royce cars allowed them to approach Turkish positions with relative impunity. Lawrence would later describe this as 'fighting deluxe'. Joyce is shown here in uniform with Arab headdress. Lawrence had long since adopted Arab robes for desert work and he is dressed here in a set of robes similar to those currently on display in the Ashmolean Museum in Oxford.

Lawrence left Aqaba on 24 October, and he and his party traced a long circuitous route to Azrak in order to avoid Turkish detection. If detected, he hoped that the chosen route would conceal their ultimate objective. At Azrak they recruited the further men required, but things also began to change for the worse. While Lawrence's Aqaba raid had been blessed with good fortune, the raid on the Yarmuk Valley was cursed with bad luck. Abd al-Qadir and his men disappeared during the night of 4–5 November, and it was feared that he had gone to warn the Turks. Lawrence's original objective (Jisr al-Hemmi) was in a location where the population was pro-Turkish, and Arab leaders told him that it could not be successfully attacked. He then chose to attack a lesser objective, the bridge at Tel ash-Shebab.

The actual raid itself took place during the night of 7–8 November 1917. Having approached as silently as possible, a local farmer fired upon Lawrence and his men, taking them for Arab raiders. Thereafter the raid descended into near farce. Noise gave away their position as a tribesman dropped his rifle and alerted a Turkish sentry, just as Lawrence was creeping forwards to plant explosives on the railway. Other sentries along the line also began to fire and Lawrence's party scattered into the darkness, dropping their explosives and equipment as they fled. The machine-gun team that was supposed to provide covering fire was in the process of moving their gun and could not open fire. On reassembling his party Lawrence found that he no longer had enough explosives to blow the bridge. As they retreated into the night, he could hear the artillery of the British offensive, which seemed to further signal his failure. During the retreat to Azrak, Lawrence did manage to destroy two culverts on the line near Minifir and to destroy the train of the commander of the Ottoman VIII Corps. While this was some measure of success, it was small consolation to him for the botched raid on the Yarmuk Valley bridges.

It is known that Lawrence returned to Azrak on 12 November, but the days that followed (14–22 November) remain something of a mystery. According to his own account in *Seven Pillars of Wisdom* he left to reconnoitre Dera'a, which was a significant Turkish garrison and a major junction on the

Lawrence photographed with his bodyguard in Aqaba in 1918. These were often recruited from the Agayl tribe. (IWM Q59576)

Hejaz Railway. While he was there Lawrence claimed he was taken prisoner and beaten and tortured, his attempt to pass himself off as a Circassian having failed. This ill treatment was followed, he later wrote, by being raped by the Turkish commander. The episode has remained one of the most controversial in Lawrence's story. Later biographers have tended to cast doubt on his account in *Seven Pillars of Wisdom*. Michael Asher in particular, a former soldier and desert traveller himself and author of *Lawrence: the uncrowned king of Arabia*, has highlighted discrepancies between Lawrence's diary entries and *Seven Pillars of Wisdom*. It is certain that Lawrence returned to Aqaba on 25 November, and there remains considerable doubt as to whether he could have travelled from Azrak to Dera'a and then from Azrak to Aqaba in the time available. The whole Dera'a episode as described in *Seven Pillars of Wisdom* remains, therefore, a point of contention among Lawrence biographers and enthusiasts alike. It has further fuelled debates on issues such as Lawrence's sexuality, as well as the motivations for his alleged post-war masochistic practices.

Lawrence also later suggested that, on his return to Aqaba, he recruited a bodyguard of 90 men, mostly Agayl. Closer examination of his diaries suggests that he had begun recruiting this bodyguard beforehand and that it never numbered more than a dozen or so men, although the total number who had served him in this capacity by the end of the war was around 90. Mounted on camels chosen and paid for by Lawrence, he kept this cohort of hard-fighters and hard-riders around him for the remainder of the war.

It is certain that Lawrence expected some form of rebuke for the failure of the Yarmuk raid when he returned to Aqaba. To his surprise, he found that Allenby was pleased with his efforts. The British offensive had breached the Gaza–Beersheba line and Lawrence's raid had succeeded in diverting some Turkish troops from the front. British troops had taken Jerusalem

Rolls-Royce armoured cars, Talbot cars and Ford cars were also allocated to the Arab Northern Army, providing both mobility and firepower for operations throughout 1918. These were armed with machine guns and 10-pdr guns. (IWM Q59529)

on 9 December, and in the official film footage of Allenby entering the city Lawrence can be seen in the background – a short, smiling figure in an ill-fitting uniform.

Final campaigns, 1917–18

The final months of 1917 were difficult for Lawrence and the other officers of the British mission. The Arab Northern Army had been considerably reinforced in November 1917 with the arrival of a squadron of Rolls-Royce armoured cars and Talbot cars mounted with 10-pdr guns. Ford light cars also formed part of this new mobile squadron. In terms of artillery, a battery of French mountain guns had been added, and these would be commanded by Capitaine Pisani of the French mission. These additions offered huge potential in terms of mobility and firepower, and in the closing months of 1917 British officers experimented in driving these cars in wadis and over the rough terrain in the region of Aqaba. They found that they performed well, and Lawrence would later record that, over certain terrain, the armoured cars could travel at up to 115km/h (70mph). Since October, parties had explored the route to the north-east of Aqaba, laying in fuel and water depots and marking out temporary airfields. The scene now seemed to be set for a new phase of the Arab Revolt, which would carry Feisal's army to Palestine and ultimately Syria.

Despite these positive developments, Lawrence also found a growing discontent among the Arab leaders. The new Bolshevik government in Russia had disclosed the full details of the Sykes-Picot Agreement, and he found that his assurances fell increasingly on deaf ears. To compound these difficulties, the Balfour Declaration of November 1917, which promised a Jewish homeland in Palestine, caused further disharmony in the Arab Army. Aware of these difficulties, Cemal Pasha made overtures to the Arab leaders and promised them both money and an amnesty. A Turkish train ambushed north of al 'Ula in November was found to be carrying over £24,000 in gold, and Lawrence feared that this was intended to buy back Arab leaders. In a series of difficult meetings Lawrence tried to reassure Feisal, and contact was made with Sharif Hussein. Arab doubts were somewhat offset by the publication of President Woodrow Wilson's

Opposite:

Around midday on 25 January 1918, Arab scouts reported the approach of Turkish forces along the Kerak road, heading in the direction of Tafila. This force of around 1,000 troops was commanded by Lt. Col. Hamid Bey and it included two Skoda mountain howitzers and over 20 machine guns and light machine guns. Lawrence and Emir Zeid had around 600 tribesmen, one mountain gun and 13 machine guns and light machine guns.

1. The battle developed around a series of ridges to the east of Tafila. Arab forces were reinforced along this line as the Ottoman brigade advanced to contact. Between 1300hrs and 1400hrs Turkish troops occupied these ridges and deployed their supporting weapons in a commanding position.

2. Lawrence decided to withdraw his forces to a position farther to the west, which he later referred to as the 'reserve ridge'. In the hours that followed a fierce firefight developed between the two forces.

3. The turning point in this action came after 1600hrs when a party of around 100 tribesmen began to advance from El 'Eime, to the north. They attacked the Turkish right flank and rear. Around 1620hrs Emir Rasim put in a further flanking attack, charging in a wide sweep into the Turkish left. Lawrence immediately followed this by leading a frontal attack. Faced with attacks on three sides, the Turkish force lost its cohesion and began to retreat back along the Kerak road.

The battle of Tafila, 25 January 1918

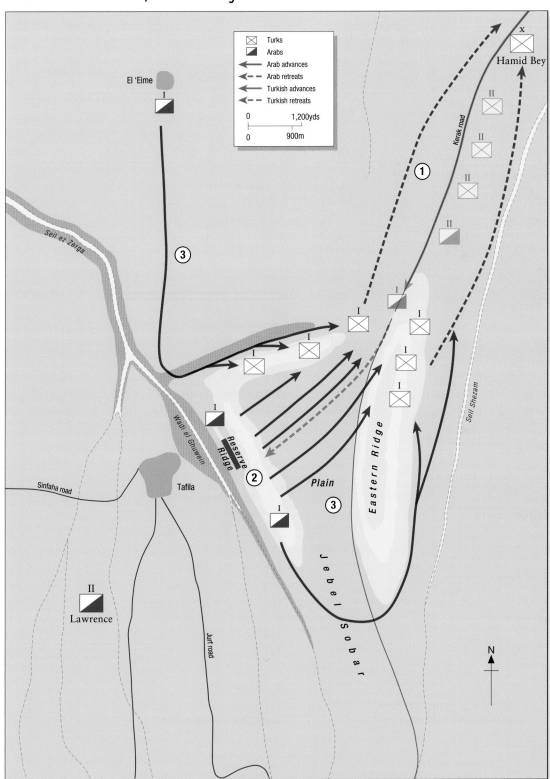

Turks

Arabs

Arab advances

Arab retreats

Turkish advances

Turkish retreats

| 0 | 1,200yds |
| 0 | 900m |

El 'Eime

Seil ez Zerga

Kerak road

Hamid Bey

Seil Shezam

Sinfaha road

Wadi el Ghuwein

Tafila

Reserve Ridge

Plain

Eastern Ridge

Jebel Sobar

Jurf road

Lawrence

N

General Sir Edmund Allenby, commander of the Egyptian Expeditionary Force from June 1917. Lawrence would endeavour to carry out attacks during 1918 in an effort to distract Turkish forces while Allenby carried out major offensives. (IWM Q82969)

'Fourteen Points' speech of 8 January 1918, which promised that 'other nationalities which are now under Turkish rule should be assured an undoubted security of life and an absolutely unmolested opportunity of autonomous development'. It was a noble assurance indeed, and one clung to by Arab leaders for the remainder of the war. In his heart though, Lawrence knew that these promises would be transcended by the Sykes-Picot provisions. As the war drew to a close, Lawrence would find his own sense of integrity gradually eroded, and this feeling would be exacerbated in the immediate post-war years.

In an immediate sense, Lawrence found himself responsible for an increasingly important part of the war in the Middle East. During late 1917, he and Lt. Col. Joyce experimented in the use of the armoured cars and Talbot cars, carrying out a series of raids on the Hejaz Railway. Lawrence revelled in the protection that the armoured cars offered, and realized that they could be used to suppress Turkish positions as demolitions took place on the railway. He described an attack on the Hejaz Railway north of Mudawwarah on 1 January 1918:

The Talbot battery opened the affair, coming spiritedly into action just below our point; while the three armoured cars crawled about the flanks of the Turkish earthwork like great dogs nosing out a trail. The enemy soldiers popped up their heads to gaze, and everything was very friendly and curious, till the cars slewed round their Vickers and began to spray the trenches. Then the Turks, realizing it was an attack, got down behind their parapets and fired at the cars raggedly. It was about as deadly as trying to warm a rhinoceros with bird-shot.

During the early months of 1918, Lawrence and Allenby discussed the future role of the Arab Army in the coming campaign, which it was hoped would be decisive. An Arab force had captured Tafila on 16 January 1918, an important town in the wheat-growing uplands to the east of the Dead Sea. It was hoped that British forces would eventually link up with the Arab Army and form one continuous line from the sea to a point beyond the end of the Turkish left flank. If this could be achieved, Allenby was confident that the Arabs could be supplied directly and not have to rely on their current supply route, which ran back to Aqaba. Ultimately, this scenario would never be realized in 1918. The terrain, which included not only the Dead Sea but also mountains and the Sea of Galilee, served to keep the two forces apart, while Turkish counter-attacks also frustrated Allenby's designs.

The retention of Tafila presented an immediate problem as, in late January 1918, a Turkish brigade marched southwards from Kerek to retake the town. Lawrence found himself with just 600 tribesmen facing a Turkish force of around 1,000 men, composed of infantry, cavalry, two mountain guns and over 20 machine guns and light machine guns. After some skirmishing, the main battle developed during 25 January. Having advanced to contact, the Turkish forces deployed on a series of ridgelines and, having forced the Arab advance parties to retreat, it seemed certain that they would retake the town. A firefight developed between Arab and Turkish positions that lasted over two hours. The battle was finally decided by an almost simultaneous series of flanking moves by Arab horsemen. Following this, Lawrence led his contingent forward in a frontal attack, and the Turkish force disintegrated and fled. The battle of Tafila was a relatively short and confused action, but it did prove that Arab irregular troops were now confident enough to face Turkish troops in open battle. It resulted in the capture of over 250 Turkish troops and their two mountain guns. Lawrence was awarded the DSO (Distinguished Service Order) on the strength of his own report of the battle, which he later admitted had been slightly tongue-in-cheek: 'Like the battle, it was nearly-proof parody of regulation use. Headquarters loved it, and innocently, to crown the jest, offered me a decoration on the strength of it. We should have more bright beasts in the Army if each man was able without witnesses, to write his own dispatch.'

The months that followed were somewhat frustrating ones for Lawrence as plans were thwarted in various ways. Immediately after Tafila, he found that £30,000 that he had given to Emir Zeid to raise further tribal levies had disappeared – being dispensed by Zeid to friends and family. Totally disillusioned at this time, Lawrence reported to Cairo that 'these Arabs are the mostly ghastly material to build into a design'. Further tactical frustrations followed. An attempt to take Ma'an in April failed, and troops of the Arab Regular Army settled down to a siege that would last until

Captured Turkish guns at Tafila in January 1918. This was the scene of a significant victory for Arab troops. Commanded by Lawrence, they successfully opposed the advance of a Turkish brigade, defeating and routing this formation. (IWM Q59368)

23 September. Also in April, the main British effort against Amman failed. A series of raids were undertaken against the Hejaz Railway in May but repeated attacks on Mudawwarah failed to take it. It was not until 8 August 1918 that this vital station was finally taken by troops of the Imperial Camel Corps, finally cutting off rail traffic heading southwards to Medina.

Both Lawrence and Allenby hoped that combined pressure along the Turkish line would force a final collapse within a few months. Allenby planned to try to force his way through the Turkish line on a narrow front at Megiddo (see Campaign 61: *Megiddo 1918*). Having breached the line, he would exploit his success by exploiting the mobility of his Desert Mounted Corps. Air power would play a crucial role and RAF planes were tasked with bombing roads, junctions and assembly places while also attacking Turkish troops on the ground.

The Arab Northern Army was a key part of Allenby's plan. He had provided Lawrence with over 1,500 camels to move a significant part of the Arab Army from Aqaba. By the beginning of September 1918 Lawrence and Feisal had initially assembled a small but highly mobile contingent of the Arab Northern Army to the east of Dera'a at El Untaiye, but later moved it to Umm Es Suret in order to avoid attention from Turkish aircraft operating out of Dera'a. This included a battalion of Arab regular troops and also the mobile contingent of armoured cars and the Talbot battery. Attached to this force were Gurkha machine-gun teams, Capitaine Pisani's mountain-gun battery and also a detachment of the Camel Corps. Lawrence had assembled over 500 tribesmen under his personal command from tribes including the Howeitat, Bani Shakr, Rwalla and Agayl, among others. A flight of RAF Bristol F2 fighters accompanied this force, using temporary airfields from which they could operate in support.

Lawrence had agreed on a concerted programme of attacks with Allenby. These would focus on the Hejaz Railway and Turkish columns, and it was hoped that they would cause confusion on the Turkish left, keeping Turkish

The battle of Tafila, 25 January 1918

Lawrence is normally associated with the guerrilla campaign that he conducted against the Hejaz Railway, but on a number of occasions he commanded Arab forces in more conventional actions against Turkish forces. Perhaps one of the most impressive victories of the Arab Army occurred at Tafila, in modern-day Jordan, in January 1918. A force of around 600 tribesmen under the command of Lawrence and Emir Zeid opposed a Turkish brigade that was superior in numbers of men, machine guns and artillery. This action was fought between a series of ridges, and for around two hours a fierce firefight raged between the Arab and Turkish forces. Lawrence would later downplay his role in this action but it is certain that he played an active role in the fighting. He is shown here armed with an SMLE rifle, a weapon he used several times during the campaign. During the action, the Arab forces made good use of their machine guns, which included Vickers, Lewis and Hotchkiss guns. Some uniformed officers of the Regular Arab Army were also present at Tafila.

commanders off-balance and contributing to a final collapse of the enemy's cohesion. In a prelude to the main offensive, Lawrence and his force began attacking the railway on 16 September 1918, carrying out a number of raids to the north and south of Dera'a, supported by the armoured car squadron. The main offensive began on 19 September, by which time Lawrence's forces had cut the railway line, effectively isolating Dera'a. Apart from opposition from Turkish troops, most particularly the Turkish camel corps, Lawrence's force was also strafed on various occasions by Turkish and German aircraft. The combined momentum of Allenby's offensive and Lawrence's attacks was beginning to erode Turkish cohesion, and troops began to retreat on foot out of Dera'a in the days that followed.

There followed perhaps the most controversial episode of Lawrence's wartime career. On 27 September a column of around 2,000 Turkish soldiers (including 250 German and Austrian troops) retreated out of Mezerib and passed through the village of Tafas, carrying out a massacre of the village's inhabitants. Leading his force of tribesmen, Lawrence came across this scene and ordered an attack on the column, later stating that he gave a 'no prisoners' order. The events that followed remain uncertain. What is certain is that the Arab tribesmen attacked the column and cut down the majority of the Turkish soldiers. Lawrence later wrote in *Seven Pillars of Wisdom* that this was to avenge the massacre at Tafas: 'In a madness born of the horror of Tafas, we killed and killed, even blowing in the heads of the fallen and the animals.' It would also appear that around 250 troops, including Germans and Austrians, did actually surrender. Lawrence later confided to his brother Arnie that he ordered them to be machine-gunned.

Lawrence's motivations for these actions continue to be debated, but it would seem that, like so many men of his generation, years of war had eroded his humanity and, having witnessed the massacre of men, women and children at Tafas, he had no hesitation in ordering that the perpetrators be gunned down. As Turkish resistance crumbled, similar scenes repeated themselves as British and Arab troops advanced.

During those final weeks of October 1918, Ottoman power in their former territory of Syria disintegrated. Despite the general confusion, Turkish troops maintained a level of cohesion, and Lawrence and his tribal forces fought a series of actions as they pushed the Turks further northwards. By now they were joined by elements of the 4th and 5th Cavalry Divisions, and the mobility of these formations came to the fore in the final actions.

An exhausted Lawrence on the balcony of a hotel in Damascus following the capture of the city in October 1918. Lawrence witnessed the frustration of Arab aspirations for independence and left the Middle East shortly afterwards. (IWM Q73534)

As Turkish command-and-control collapsed, Turkish troops surrendered in their thousands; Allenby's Megiddo offensive had been a total success. Damascus was taken on 1 October by Arab tribesmen and British and Australian cavalry. Aleppo fell to Arab troops on 26 October, and Arab and British troops took the vital railway junction at Muslimiya on 29 October. The seizure of this junction cut the Turkish rail link to Mesopotamia. The Ottoman Empire sued for peace and was granted an armistice on 31 October. The war in the Middle East was over.

Lawrence's own war had effectively ended when he reached Damascus on 1 October. His tribesmen had continued to harass the retreating Turks but he left them to enter the town, travelling in a Rolls-Royce tender that he had named 'Blue Mist'. Lodging himself in the Victoria Hotel, he was both physically and emotionally exhausted. Damascus, the city that he had so longed to reach, was in a shambles. There was widespread disorder in the streets and essential services had broken down. Visiting the Turkish hospital, he found the abandoned sick and wounded in a pitiable state. A medical officer struck Lawrence across the face, calling him a 'bloody brute'. Lawrence later wrote that 'in my heart I felt he was right'.

The wider jubilation of the victors in Damascus was in stark contrast to Lawrence's personal feelings. At a tense meeting on 3 October, Allenby informed Feisal that he would not be allowed to become king of Syria. It would be governed by the French, under the terms of the Sykes-Picot Agreement. Any lasting illusions that both Feisal and Lawrence had were stripped away. James McBey painted a portrait of Lawrence at this time in a single sitting. He later recorded that Arab leaders came to bid farewell to Lawrence as he sat in his hotel room, kissing his hand one by one and taking their leave. The portrait (see Campaign 202: *The Arab Revolt 1916–18*) and photographs of this time show an exhausted Lawrence. Following the meeting with Feisal, Lawrence secured permission from Allenby to leave. He recorded:

Emir Feisal leaving the Victoria Hotel in Damascus on 3 October 1918, having been informed by General Allenby that he would not be allowed to govern Syria, which was ceded to France under the terms of the Sykes-Picot Agreement. (IWM Q12364)

The final campaign, 16 September to 28 October 1918

Opposite:

The final phase of General Allenby's campaign in the Middle East began on 16 September 1918 with the start of a new offensive. The Arab Northern Army under Feisal and Lawrence played a crucial role, attacking the Hejaz Railway and holding down the Turkish left flank. During the course of a few dramatic weeks they continued to move northwards as the Turkish Army fell back.

1. At the opening stage of the offensive the Arab Northern Army (numbering around 1,000 men) was based at El Umtaiye and carried out raids on the railway from 16 September, before the main offensive was launched on 19 September (the Megiddo Offensive).

2. On 27 September, Lawrence's force attacked and destroyed a retreating Turkish force at Tafas. The town of Dera'a fell later that day.

3. In cooperation with the 4th Cavalry Division, the Arab forces continued to pursue retreating Turkish forces towards Damascus, which was captured on 1 October.

4. In the weeks that followed, the retreating Ottoman forces were pursued northwards by the Arab Northern Army and by the 4th and 5th Cavalry Divisions. Aircraft of the RAF carried out a series of devastating attacks on retreating Turkish columns. Arab and British troops arrived at Aleppo on 26 October and the Ottoman government signed an armistice five days later.

When Feisal had gone, I made to Allenby the last (and also I think the first) request I ever made for myself – leave to go away. For a while he would not have it; but I reasoned, reminding him of his year-old promise, and pointing out how much easier the New Law would be if my spur were absent from the people. In the end he agreed; and then at once I knew how much I was sorry.

Lawrence left Damascus the next day and was back in Cairo by 8 October 1918. He had left that city as a mere lieutenant in 1916 but now returned as a full colonel with a DSO and a CB. General Allenby had recommended that Lawrence be given a knighthood. Despite these trappings of success, it is certain that the outcome of the revolt was a profound disappointment to him. As he later wrote, he had seen his 'dreams puffed out like candles, in the strong wind of success'.

OPPOSING COMMANDERS

One fascinating aspect of the history of the Arab Revolt is that there has been so little attention paid to the Ottoman Army and its commanders during that campaign. The literature on this subject in the English language is quite limited, although *A Military Mistory of the Ottomans: from Osman to Atatürk* (2009) by Mesut Uyar and Edward J. Erickson has gone some way towards redressing this imbalance. Lawrence himself mentions several of the Ottoman commanders in *Seven Pillars of Wisdom* and generally acknowledges that they had potential but were operating to the limit of what their dwindling military assets would allow.

It must also be said that, because of the nature of the asymmetric campaign that he waged, it was not Lawrence's practice to engage Ottoman forces in conventional battle. To gain some understanding of the quality of his opposition, one must consider how they engaged in counter-insurgency. It must also be pointed out that it is unlikely that the senior Ottoman commanders even knew of Lawrence's existence. They knew only that they were facing an Arab rebellion and that this was being assisted by

Ahmed Cemel Pasha (Büyük), governor of Ottoman Syria and commander of 4th Field Army. A politically astute general, Cemel Pasha was ultimately responsible for the campaign against Lawrence and the Arab armies. (IWM Q45339)

Allied officers and an increasing amount of Allied *matériel*. The Ottoman commanders knew that raiding parties under Arab and Allied officers were targeting their main line of communication but they did not identify a single officer as being the driving force behind this. Equally, the idea that the Turkish high command had placed a price on Lawrence's head is a total myth.

With respect to command responsibilities, the Arab Revolt took place in territory under the control of **Ahmed Cemal Pasha (Büyük[1])**. This soldier and ambitious statesman was a leading figure in the Committee of Union and Progress (CUP). Cemal Pasha had graduated from military secondary school in 1890 and from the Imperial Military Academy (Mekteb-i Harbiye) in 1893. He was commissioned as a lieutenant and selected to attend the Staff College (Erkan-ı Harbiye Mektebi), from which he graduated in 1896 as a general-staff captain.

After the Young Turk Revolution of 1908 Cemal Pasha came to prominence as the military governor of Istanbul city and, considered an expert in internal security, he was appointed as governor of Adana province during the Armenian rebellion of 1909. As a field commander he was less sure of himself, and his period as a divisional commander during the Balkan Wars was not auspicious. He took an active part in the *coup d'état* of 1913 and became one of the strongmen of the CUP dictatorship, emerging as one of the main power brokers of the Young Turk regime. He was promoted to brigadier-general, while also serving as minister of public works and minister of the Navy.

When World War I began he was appointed as the commander of 4th Field Army, headquartered in Damascus, with the rank of major-general. Once again he also filled a dual government position, being made governor of Ottoman Syria, with responsibility for the Ottoman possessions in Arabia.

---

1 'Senior' or 'greater'.

During the first years of the war he oversaw the crackdown against Syrian nationalists. Between 1914 and 1916, he organized the roundup of Syrian nationalists of the al-Fatat movement, an operation that would influence the outbreak of the Arab Revolt. Hugely ambitious, he excelled in the political power games of that turbulent period and independently commanded and governed this region during the war. In 1915 he was responsible for the unsuccessful Ottoman offensive against Suez. Despite this failure, he effectively opposed the gradual British advance through Sinai and into Palestine.

The outbreak of the Arab Revolt in 1916 created further military challenges for Ahmed Cemal Pasha and, forbidding the withdrawal of troops from Arabia, he set about trying to crush this rebellion while also maintaining forces at a huge remove. His choice of subordinates to serve in this campaign was wise indeed, and both Mehmed Cemal Pasha (Küçük[2]) and Ömer Fahrettin Pasha (Türkkan) operated effectively against Arab forces until 1918.

Ahmed Cemal Pasha (Küçük). This Ottoman general was known as 'Cemal the Lesser' to distinguish him from his senior commander of the same name. Photographed here with his children in Jerusalem in 1917, he commanded the 1st Kuvve-i-Mürettebe, which was based at Ma'an and played a major role in operations against the Arab Revolt. (Library of Congress, Washington)

Ahmed Cemal Pasha lost his local dominance in 1918 with the arrival of German General von Falkenhayn, and the loss of the Yıldırım Army Group staff to his area of operations. It is often debated whether his insistence on maintaining Ottoman troops in Arabia adversely affected the outcome of the campaign in Palestine. If evacuated from Arabia, Ottoman troops could well have reinforced his 4th Field Army. Yet he was also aware that withdrawal from Arabia would spell the end of Ottoman power there and, always sensitive to wider political ramifications, this was something he refused to countenance. He later conspired against Enver Pasha, and after the war went to both Russia and Afghanistan. He was assassinated by Armenian gunmen on 22 July 1922.

The town of Ma'an (in modern-day Jordan) was situated at a crucial location on the Hejaz Railway and, as the campaign against the railway intensified, it became a major centre for Ottoman operations. The Ottoman commander there, **Mehmed Cemal Pasha (Küçük)**, played a major role in operations against the Arab Revolt while also striving to keep the railway line open to allow resupply of the garrison farther south at Medina.

Mehmed Cemal Pasha had graduated from the Imperial Military Academy in 1895, being commissioned as a lieutenant. He was later selected for staff training and graduated from Staff College in 1898 as a general-staff captain. As a young general-staff officer he had gained a wide experience serving in different corners of the Ottoman Empire. He showed extreme zeal against Kurdish rebels in Dersim (Eastern Anatolia), for which he was decorated. He turned out to be equally talented in diplomatic missions, and he served in various border-dispute commissions. He was one of the few divisional commanders to emerge from the Balkan Wars with his reputation intact.

---

2 'Junior' or 'lesser'.

On the outbreak of World War I he was promoted to brigadier-general and assigned command of VIII Army Corps, which was tasked with attacking the Suez Canal in 1915. His later wartime career was made difficult because of Ahmed Cemal Pasha (Büyük)'s highly centralized command style. This was why he was known among brother officers as 'Küçük Cemal Pasha', literally 'Cemal the Lesser', although presumably not to his face. With his headquarters at Ma'an, he commanded the 1st Kuvve-i-Mürettebe, a highly mobile mixed force that operated against Arab forces in the desert. It also fell to him to garrison blockhouses along the Hejaz Railway and repair any demolitions within his operating area. Mehmed Cemal Pasha carried out these tasks very effectively, and recent archaeological excavations have revealed that Ma'an was protected by a network of elaborate entrenchments. He defended Ma'an against a major attack by Arab Regular Army forces and tribesmen in April 1917 and the town was not evacuated until September 1918. Throughout his period of command at Ma'an he used his limited air assets very effectively, with air attacks on the Arab base at Aqaba occurring on a regular basis.

Later in the war he found his role diminished during the Palestine campaign because of the presence of German officers such as Kress von Kressenstein. He was finally assigned as the commanding general of 4th Field Army (relieving Büyük Cemal Pasha) on 17 January 1918 and was promoted to major-general in July.

Perhaps the best-known Ottoman commander during the Arab Revolt is **Ömer Fahrettin Pasha (Türkkan)**, who commanded the garrison at Medina during the Arab Revolt. In English-language sources he is also often referred to as Fakhreddin or Fakhri Pasha. He was born in Ruse in Ottoman Bulgaria in 1868 and had also passed through the Imperial Military Academy and the Staff College. He graduated from Staff College in 1891 as a general-staff captain. As a young general-staff officer he served in garrisons in different corners of the Ottoman Empire and, in addition to regular staff jobs and field commands, he served on several border-dispute commissions. His record in the Balkan Wars was undistinguished but at the beginning of World War I he held divisional command. He was assigned to command XVIII Army Corps, while also serving as second-in-command of 4th Field Army. In this capacity he acted as deputy to Cemal Pasha Büyük.

Ömer Fahrettin Pasha's appointment to command at Medina was very much a last-minute one, but it proved to be extremely appropriate. Following the outbreak of the revolt, he not only organized the city's defences but immediately set out to secure the Hejaz Railway. In late 1916 he set out to crush the revolt and retake the towns of Yanbu and Rabegh, setting out with a force of two brigades and advancing towards the main Arab forces. This is a task that he came extremely close to accomplishing, and he might have crushed the revolt while it was till in its infancy but for the arrival of Royal Navy forces and Egyptian troops. Logistical factors also played their part, and he returned to Medina in early 1917. For the remainder of the war he maintained a stubborn defence of Medina, making huge efforts to keep the railway line open, as it was his major means of resupply and reinforcement. He was not, however, totally reliant on the railway, as he still obtained food supplies from Ibn Rashid's Shammar tribe, who were loyal to Ottoman rule.

While the three officers described above were the senior Ottoman commanders in Lawrence's area of operation, he never engaged them directly as this was not the type of war that Lawrence was waging. To a certain extent, therefore, it could be argued that Lawrence had few Ottoman commanders who directly opposed him. This was the nature of his war. He measured success not by conventional military standards, but sought to destroy the Ottoman capacity for war through irregular action. As for the senior Ottoman commanders described here, they were never in a position to engage Lawrence directly but concerned themselves with trying to counter Arab attacks and overcome damage to the Hejaz Railway.

Like so many involved in the Lawrence story, the names and qualities of the Ottoman officers who opposed the Arab Revolt have largely been forgotten. From what we can gather, it would seem that they were experienced, intelligent and tenacious, qualities that were common to Ottoman soldiers throughout World War I.

INSIDE THE MIND

From obscure beginnings in every sense, Lawrence has emerged as one of the iconic figures of the 20th century. In a purely military sense he played a major role during World War I. As a military commander he had an absolute grasp of guerrilla warfare and could translate this into appropriate action and express it with the written word. The fact that his writings are returned to again and again is proof of the accuracy of his theories on irregular warfare. It was this instinct that coalesced with his knowledge of the tribes and terrain of Arabia and allowed him to operate with success during World War I. His success at operating in the desert with irregular forces, supplemented by light armour and artillery, would be built upon by desert explorers during the 1920s and 1930s. In conjunction, these methods would be used by special forces, such as the Long Range Desert Group and the SAS, during desert operations in World War II. As a result, Lawrence remains one of the most influential figures in guerrilla warfare and the development of desert-warfare tactics.

The neatest summation of his own art of war is contained in Chapter XXXIII of *Seven Pillars of Wisdom*, which describes how he spent a period bed-ridden

A bust of Lawrence by Eric Kennington. The original bust is in St Paul's Cathedral in London. Several copies were later made and this example is in the chapel of Jesus College, Oxford, where Lawrence had been an undergraduate. (Author's photograph)

because of illness in early 1917. During this period he developed his ideas on how the campaign should be conducted. He estimated Turkish strengths and weaknesses and assessed what advantages the Arab forces had over the Turks. His final assessment contains many principles still recognized by students of asymmetric warfare. Lawrence rejected the offensive mindset so typified by commanders on the Western Front. The Turks, he realized, were bound to protect territory in Arabia, as well as the Hejaz Railway. Their corresponding trade-off was in mobility, as they remained tied to vulnerable lines of communication. The Arabs on the other had could range far afield and wage a war of surprise attacks. A reasonably modest supply of machine guns and explosives would allow them to increase their advantage. Lawrence neatly summed up his ideas:

Lawrence was an inspirational subject for many artists. This portrait by Augustus John was completed in 1919 and is part of the Tate Collection. (Tate Gallery, London)

Most wars were wars of contact, both forces striving into touch to avoid tactical surprise. Ours should be a war of detachment. We were to contain the enemy by the silent threat of a vast unknown desert, not disclosing ourselves till we attacked. The attack would be nominal, directed not against him, but against his stuff; so it would not seek either his strength or his weakness, but his most accessible material.

As a commander of this kind of guerrilla war, he also realized the advantages offered by the armoured-car squadron and the use of airpower. The use of these in conjunction with his tribal forces meant that a relatively small force could bring significant firepower to bear on the enemy. He would use such assets to great effect in the later stages of the war.

Above all, Lawrence was a desert commander, and his experience of this difficult terrain allowed him to develop methods to survive and travel in it. He knew that prudent use of wells (and later supply depots) would allow him to cover vast distances. He chose his travelling camels with care and later would pay attention to the maintenance of motor vehicles. Lawrence ultimately used the desert to his advantage. By knowing that he could survive during long expeditions, he could travel through desert considered totally inhospitable by the enemy and then emerge from it with considerable tactical advantage to attack his target. This was the basic principle behind the Aqaba raid, and he would this tactic again and again.

Lawrence was unwilling to sustain unnecessary casualties, realizing that casualties in his Arab forces would have wider ramifications in Arab society. Lawrence's whole attitude to bloodshed is still debated. Some incidents in the war, such as that at Tafas in 1918, suggest that the war had hardened him and that he accepted the necessity of bloodshed. In private letters he was more forthcoming. In a letter to a friend (Edward Leeds), he wrote: 'This killing and killing of Turks is horrible. When you charge in at the finish and find them all over the place in bits, and still alive many of them, and know that you have done hundreds in the same way before and must do hundreds more if you can.'

Lawrence's relationship with his fellow officers was often tense, and in that sense he did not conform to the usual standards we would expect from a wartime leader. There were various sources of tension – the proposed use of the Imperial Camel Corps being one example. Also, in 1918, Lawrence effectively imploded a plan for a large raid being prepared by Joyce and Young, having got permission from Cairo for his own alternative plan. Convinced of the soundness of his own judgements, Lawrence was far from a team player.

The fact that Lawrence had no pre-war military experience ultimately acted to his advantage in the desert campaign. He came with no preconceived notions as to how the war should be run. He brought his knowledge of the tribes and the terrain and used them to his advantage in the field. Some have dismissed him as merely a gifted, or lucky, amateur, but in truth Lawrence was a man of vast intelligence. As a result he could formulate his own doctrine of desert guerrilla warfare while actually in the field. In recent years his writings and experiences have been returned to again in light of more recent conflicts in Iraq and Afghanistan. Such a process calls for caution. Lawrence's experience related to a very specific context and time. It would be optimistic to believe that he could offer a template applicable to modern circumstances. It should also be remembered that Lawrence saw the war from the viewpoint of the insurgent, and modern proponents of counter-insurgency need to realize that when studying him. However, as an advocate of asymmetric warfare, Lawrence still has much to offer the modern reader. Lawrence's story also confirms that, even in the vast impersonal conflict that was World

Lawrence accompanied the delegation of Emir Feisal to the Paris Peace Conference in 1919. Despite his efforts on their behalf, few of the promises made to the Arab leaders would be kept. Feisal would later become king of Iraq, under the terms of the British mandate. (IWM Q55581)

War I, an individual officer could make a difference, and by his actions influence the outcome of an entire campaign.

WHEN WAR IS DONE

Shortly after Lawrence's death, Lord Allenby summed up his wartime career, stating: 'He was a shy and retiring scholar, archaeologist, and philosopher swept by the tide of war in to a position undreamt of. He had a genius for leadership. Above all men he had no regard for ambition, but did his duty as he saw it.' (*Guardian*, 19 May 1935). This was a remarkably accurate

National Hero. Following the successful screenings in London of a series of films by Lowell Thomas on the Arab Revolt, Lawrence became a popular hero. He later posed for further publicity photographs, of which this is one, and saw his fame spread internationally. (IWM Q46064)

assessment, and, although Lawrence is often accused of having an overweening ambition, it would seem that the pressures of post-war public attention came to be unbearable for him. His virtual withdrawal from life and his rejection of career possibilities in various fields could be seen as proof that the burden of the 'Lawrence Myth' was too much for him. Like many 'celebrities' since, while he initially seems to have enjoyed the public attention, it soon became burdensome. His decision to abandon whole facets of his life only served to further fuel public interest, guaranteeing that the myth would outlive him.

Despite his misgivings about the possibilities of a just post-war settlement in the Middle East, Lawrence remained committed to the Arab cause, refusing the offer of a knighthood in protest at the way the Arabs had been treated. In 1919 he accompanied Prince Feisal to the Paris Peace Conference as part of the Arab delegation. The terms of the wartime Sykes-Picot Agreement ensured that Arab representations were in vain, and the former

Above: In 1921 Lawrence formed part of the British delegation at the Cairo Conference, during which a settlement was reached on the growing discontent in the Middle East. (IWM Q60171)

Ottoman territories of the Middle East were divided up between Britain and France. During 1919 Lawrence had begun writing his memoir of the campaign, which he compiled from his wartime notebooks and journals. This would later be published as *Seven Pillars of Wisdom* (see p. 59 below). Redrafting of this work would continue in phases for several years to come. In June 1919 he was made a research fellow of All Souls College in Oxford and it seemed as though Lawrence would return to his pre-war career path of historian and archaeologist.

A series of events were soon to make him a household name in Britain, and his reputation soon spread beyond its shores. The birth of Lawrence's wider public celebrity came in August 1919 when Lowell Thomas opened a show in Covent Garden entitled *With Allenby in Palestine*. Thomas had toured the Middle East during the war and had accumulated a store of film footage and still photographs, some of it showing Lawrence. The initial show included a lecture, slideshow and also music and dance. Thomas quickly realized that his audience was fascinated with Lawrence's story. He held meetings with Lawrence, who posed for further photographs. Thomas' new show was entitled *With Allenby in Palestine and Lawrence in Arabia*. It played to packed crowds in London

Right: Lawrence is photographed here at the RAF base at Miramshah on the North-West Frontier. This posting to an area bordering Afghanistan led to rumours in the press that he was engaged in spying activity. (IWM Q115096)

From 1932 Lawrence was involved in the development of high-speed RAF rescue craft such as this example. These would later operate very effectively in World War II, rescuing downed aircrew. (IWM CH001687).

and then went on tour around Britain. By 1920 Lawrence had ceased to be one of the less well-known heroes of the war and had been elevated to the status of living legend. The reasons for this have been long debated, but, after years of dehumanized warfare and anonymous death on the Western Front, it is safe to say that this charismatic individual held both a fascination and an appeal for the general public.

While Lawrence has since been criticized for how he played to this public and press attention, it can also be shown that he tried to use his celebrity to further the Arab cause and urge the fulfillment of wartime promises that had been made to Arab leaders. Iraq had descended into rebellion in 1920 after the British had been given the administration of the country under the terms of their mandate. Lawrence was increasingly vocal on British policy there. On 2 August 1920 he wrote in *The Times*:

Clouds Hill in Dorset. Lawrence retired from the RAF in 1935 and went to live in this isolated cottage. (Photograph courtesy of Peter Leney, T. E. Lawrence Society)

> The people of England have been led in Mesopotamia into a trap from which it will be hard to escape with dignity and honour. They have been tricked into it by a steady withholding of information. The Baghdad communiqués are belated, insincere, incomplete. Things have been far worse than we have been told, our administration more bloody and inefficient than the public knows. It is a disgrace to our imperial record, and may soon be too inflamed for any ordinary cure. We are to-day not far from a disaster.

Lawrence continued in this tone, condemning French military actions in Syria. In 1921 he was invited to join the Colonial Office as an advisor on Arab affairs. In this capacity he accompanied Winston Churchill to the Cairo Conference in March 1921, being one of the 40 experts (or 'forty thieves' as Churchill referred to them) who were assembled in the hope of reaching agreement on the administration of the mandated territories. The conference saw the successful conclusion of an Anglo-Iraqi treaty and the installation of Feisal as king of Iraq. Despite being threatened by various coups and upheavals, this form of government would survive in Iraq until the Ba'athist revolution of 1958.

On his return to England it would seem that Lawrence was increasingly aware that he would never be successful in forcing a just settlement in Arabia, regardless of how well he used his public persona and utilized the press. In 1922 he resigned from all offices and, assuming the name 'J. H. Ross', he joined the RAF as an enlisted man. Discovery by the press forced him out of the RAF, but he then enlisted in the Tank Corps in 1923, this time having changed his name to 'T. E. Shaw'. In 1925 he returned to the RAF and would continue to serve as an enlisted man until his retirement in 1935.

This rejection by Lawrence of career, public life and even his own identity could not have been foreseen by many at the time. In 1922 several career paths lay open to him but he rejected them all and sought obscurity in the RAF. Debate has continued ever since as to his motivations. Some have argued that it was a publicity stunt or a final protest as to the treatment of the Arabs. Others have reasoned that it was a result of wartime stress or was because of a wider disillusionment with British politics and society. Issues such as difficulties with his own sexuality and identity have also been offered. In any event, the T. E. Lawrence that had so captivated the world's press and public since 1919 had withdrawn into a more private world. He would later state that he had 'backed out of the

Lawrence had a life-long passion for speed and, while in the RAF, he owned a series of powerful Brough motorcycles. It was whilst riding such a machine that he was fatally injured in an accident in 1935.
(Bodleian Library, Oxford)

Alec Guinness, David Lean and Peter O'Toole on the set of *Lawrence of Arabia*. At over 6ft tall, O'Toole was perhaps an unlikely Lawrence, but his performance captured many of the complexities of the man.
(Author's collection)

A poster advertising *Lawrence of Arabia*. While Lawrence had been the subject of dramatic works before, this film was a huge international success and reintroduced Lawrence to a wider audience. (Author's collection)

race and sat down among people who were not racing'. Despite this rather romantic summation, his letters to close friends show that he found life as a ranker difficult as he adjusted to living among fellow servicemen who were, to say the least, 'earthy'.

Living as unobtrusively as possible in a succession of RAF stations, he still managed to attract a certain amount of press attention. His posting to Miramshah on the North-West Frontier of India in 1928 generated press speculation that he was somehow involved in espionage work against Afghanistan. While serving in the RAF, Lawrence (or Shaw, as he now was) continued to work on *Seven Pillars of Wisdom* and other literary projects. He completed a translation of Homer's *Odyssey* in 1932 and began a memoir of his life in the RAF. This would later be published as *The Mint*. He also served as a contributor to the *Encyclopedia Britannica*.

Lawrence had also always loved speed. He indulged in this passion through owning a series of Brough motorcyles during the 1920s and 1930s. He later described his habit of driving these powerful motorcycles at high speeds as 'voluntary danger'. Lawrence also loved flying and, during the war and after, he made many aerial trips. He never learned to fly but did later work on the development of high-speed RAF rescue boats. Throughout his years in the RAF he maintained his correspondence with a vast array of friends and acquaintances.

In February 1935 Lawrence retired from the RAF, beginning a new phase of press speculation as to what his future would hold. He now lived at Clouds Hill in Dorset, a cottage that he had bought previously. On the morning of 13 May he was involved in a motorcycle accident while returning to Clouds Hill from Bovington Camp. Lawrence sustained serious head injuries and died six days later on 19 May 1935. His funeral was attended by a large crowd, which included fellow servicemen and also more prominent figures such as Winston Churchill, Siegfried Sassoon, General A. P. Wavell, Colonel Newcombe, Sir Ronald Storrs and Lady Astor. His brother,

Lawrence in civilian clothes during his final years in the RAF. (IWM Q113749)

Arnold Lawrence, led the mourners and received a telegram from King George V, which stated: 'Your brother's name will live in history and the King gratefully recognises his distinguished services to his country and feels that it is tragic that the end should have come in this manner to a life still so full of promise.'

Yet Lawrence's death was not the end of his story. Since 1935 he has remained a subject of fascination for scholars, soldiers and the public at large. This fascination has been fuelled by the gradual publication of his own works and also by an ever-growing literature, with hardly a year passing without the publication of some new work on his life or the Arab Revolt. In recent years the campaigns in Iraq and Afghanistan have caused a new generation of scholars and soldiers to return to his life and works in an effort to gain insights into the problems of insurrection and counter-insurgency in the Arab world. Prominent among modern commentators are David Kilcullen and Rory Stewart, who both refer to the influence of Lawrence in their works.

Lawrence's life has also always provided inspiration for works of fiction and drama. In 1960 Terence Rattigan's play *Ross* was greeted with acclaim on the London stage, with Alec Guinness in the title role. But it was David Lean's 1962 film *Lawrence of Arabia* that reintroduced Lawrence to the wider world. With Peter O'Toole as an unlikely Lawrence (at over 6ft, O'Toole was much taller than the real Lawrence), the film became a cinematic sensation, despite its historical simplifications and omissions. Lawrence has since been portrayed on stage and screen by many actors, including Simon Ward and Ralph Fiennes. He was even included in the 1992 television series *The Young Indiana Jones Chronicles*.

Separating Lawrence from his own legend is a difficult and often contentious business. It could be argued that we move further from the true

Lawrence with each passing year. A collector, who recently found a major
piece of Lawrence memorabilia, later confessed that he had thought that
Lawrence of Arabia was merely a fictional character! It would seem that the
legend has largely transcended the man.

A LIFE IN WORDS

Lawrence led a life that was far from ordinary, and during his own lifetime
he saw the beginnings of what has become a veritable literary industry
based on the subject of his life and the Arab Revolt. For many readers, his
own writings still serve as an introduction to Lawrence and the desert
campaigns. While still at college, he had planned to write a history of seven
great cities in the Middle East and the working title of this study was
Seven Pillars of Wisdom. While he later abandoned this project, he retained
the title and decided to use it for his epic World War I memoir. It is obvious
from his letters that he found this a difficult task, a fact compounded by
him losing a draft of the book in 1919 while changing trains at Reading
railway station. Despite these difficulties, he would bring out three versions
of his memoir during his lifetime, constantly revising the text. In 1922 he
printed just eight copies of what has come to be known as the 'Oxford Text'

or '1922 edition'. Lawrence brought out a limited, subscribers-only edition, in 1926, of which only 100 went on public sale. An abridged version entitled *The Revolt in the Desert* was published in 1927 and this was greeted with both critical approval and public enthusiasm. A further edition of *Seven Pillars of Wisdom* was published after his death in 1935 for public consumption. This edition has remained in print ever since. It was not until 1997 that the unabridged 1922 edition was finally published on a commercial level.

An effigy of Lawrence in Arab robes. Carved by Eric Kennington, it was placed in the church of St Martin's in Wareham, Dorset. (Photography courtesy of Ian Heritage, T. E. Lawrence Society)

Lawrence's account of his experiences in the RAF, *The Mint*, was printed in a private version of just 50 copies. Because of what Jeremy Wilson has referred to as the 'barrack-room language' used, and also the realistic depictions of barracks life, this was not published until 1955, 20 years after his death. Even at that time the publishers issued an expurgated version with passages that could have caused offence omitted. In 1936 Lawrence's college thesis on Crusader castles was published and has since been republished.

The public's fascination with Lawrence throughout the 1920s and 1930s was fed by the world's press. As a result, it is not surprising that his every action seemed to spawn newspaper, magazine and journal articles all over the world. Many of these survive in libraries and they make a fascinating study in themselves. Lawrence's untimely death in 1935 sparked a further flurry in the international press, and the *Guardian* of 15 May 1935 set the general tone when it remarked: 'Tragic … that such a remarkable career should have been ended by a simple road accident.' In the days that followed, journalists scrabbled to obtain quotes from former colleagues, the most sought-after being Field Marshal Lord Allenby. In a speech in London, Allenby remarked:

> His cooperation was marked by the utmost loyalty and I never had anything but praise

Right: A Lawrence artefact: one of his head ropes. This example is in the collection of the Imperial War Museum in London. Other artefacts associated with Lawrence are held in various museums and private collections, and memorabilia connected with 'Lawrence of Arabia' remains highly collectable. (IWM UNI12240)

for his work, which, indeed, was invaluable throughout the campaign. He was the mainspring of the Arab movement and knew their language, their manners and their mentality. He shared with the Arabs their hardships and dangers. Among these desert raiders there was none who would not have willingly died for his chief. In fact not a few lost their lives in devotion to him and in defence of his person.

It was a neat summation of Lawrence's career, and generations of scholars have been either supporting this thesis, or re-examining it, ever since.

Lawrence's life has provided rich material for biographers since the 1920s. While he was still living, both Robert Graves and Basil Liddell Hart wrote biographies of Lawrence and had the advantage of interviewing him and also other veterans of the desert campaign. Lawrence's biographers have included scholars, soldiers, journalists, Arabists, psychologists and many others. They have initiated debates about various facets of Lawrence's character – his relationship with his mother, his dealings with the Arabs, his truthfulness regarding events in his life, his sexuality and so on. Few have debated his natural ability as a guerrilla leader or his passion for the Arab cause. Some of the more readily available biographies are listed in the 'Further Reading' section below, but this list is by no means exhaustive. The authorized biography by Jeremy Wilson, published in 1989, is still an essential source for those wishing to approach this complex individual.

Another major resource for anyone interested in Lawrence is his letter collections. While these are held in public and private archives in various locations, edited collections are also generally available. Throughout his life Lawrence was a prodigious letter-writer. In order to keep in touch with his wide circle of friends and associates, he often wrote many letters a day. His list of correspondents spanned all sections of society and included military figures, politicians, writers, artists and servicemen from his time in the RAF. His correspondents included Winston Churchill, Lord Trenchard, Noël Coward, George Bernard Shaw and his wife Charlotte, E. M. Forster, Augustus John and many others. For those seeking an insight into his life, career and character they are invaluable. In 1938 Edward Garnett published an edited collection of Lawrence letters as *The Letters of T. E. Lawrence*. Malcolm Brown, a long-time scholar of Lawrence, has edited further comprehensive collections of letters, which were published in London (1988) and New York (1989). A more recent collection was edited by Malcolm Brown and published as *Lawrence of Arabia: the selected letters* (2007).

There are various societies and associations across the world that dedicate their activities to examining Lawrence's life. Prominent among these is the Oxford-based T. E. Lawrence Society (http://telsociety.org.uk/telsociety/index.htm). Online sources are numerous indeed and it would be impossible to list them all. One of the more comprehensive of these is the T. E. Lawrence Studies website (http://telawrence.net/telawrencenet/index.htm), which is associated with Lawrence's official biographer, Jeremy Wilson.

FURTHER READING

Asher, Michael, *Lawrence: the uncrowned king of Arabia*, Penguin: London, 1998

Barr, James, *Setting the Desert on Fire: T. E. Lawrence and Britain's secret war in Arabia*, Bloomsbury: London, 2006

Brown, Malcolm, *The Letters of T. E. Lawrence*, Dent: London, 1988

——, *T. E. Lawrence: the selected letters*, Norton: New York, 1989 and Oxford University Press: Oxford, 1991

——, *Secret Despatches from Arabia and Other Writings*, Bellew Publishing: London, 1991

——, *T. E. Lawrence,* British Library Historic Lives series, the British Library: London, 2003

——, *Lawrence of Arabia: the life, the legend*, Thames & Hudson: London, 2005

——, *Lawrence of Arabia: the selected letters*, Max, an imprint of Little Books: London, 2007

Garnett, Edward, *The Letters of T. E. Lawrence*, Doubleday, Doran & Company: London, 1938

Graves, Robert, *Lawrence and the Arabs*, Jonathan Cape: London, 1927

Hyde, H. Montgomery, *Solitary in the Ranks: T. E. Lawrence as airman and private soldier*, Constable: London, 1977

James, Lawrence, *The Golden Warrior: the life and legend of Lawrence of Arabia*, Abacus: London, 1990

The Journal of the T. E. Lawrence Society

Kilcullen, David, *The Accidental Guerrilla: fighting small wars in the midst of a big one*, Hurst & Company: London, 2009

Lawrence, T. E., *Seven Pillars of Wisdom*, privately printed in 1922 and 1926, first public edition, Jonathan Cape: London, 1935

——, *The Revolt in the Desert*, first edition, Jonathan Cape: London, 1927

——, *The Mint*, privately printed limited edition (50 copies) 1936, first public edition, Jonathan Cape: London, 1955 (in both expurgated and unexpurgated formats)

Leclerc, Christophe, *Avec Lawrence en Arabie: la mission militaire française au Hezaz, 1916–20*, Harmattan: Paris, 1998

Liddell Hart, Basil, *T. E. Lawrence: in Arabia and after*, Jonathan Cape: London, 1934

Mack, John E., *The Prince of our Disorder*, Little, Brown & Company: London, 1978

Mohs, Polly A., *Military Intelligence and the Arab Revolt: the first modern intelligence war*, Routledge: London, 2008

Mousa, Suleiman, *T. E. Lawrence: an Arab view*, Oxford University Press: Oxford, 1966

Murphy, David, Campaign 202: *The Arab Revolt 1916–18: Lawrence sets Arabia ablaze*, Osprey Publishing: Oxford, 2008

Nicolle, David, Men-at-Arms 208: *Lawrence and the Arab Revolts*, Osprey Publishing: Oxford, 1989

Tabachnik, Stephen E. (ed.), *The T. E. Lawrence Puzzle*, University of Georgia Press: Athens, GA, 1984

Uyar, Mesut and Erickson, Edward J., *A Military History of the Ottomans: from Osman to Atatürk*, Praeger Security International: Santa Barbara, CA, 2009

Wilson, Jeremy, *Lawrence of Arabia: the authorized biography*, William Heinemann: London, 1989

INDEX